Communication

Colonization and the Making of a Discipline

Amardo J. Rodriguez

ISBN: 0692239081
ISBN 13: 9780692239087

Public Square Press
309 Fayette Drive
Fayetteville, NY 13066
USA

For

Joshua & Jordan

Contents

One

On History and Conquest

I freed a thousand slaves. I could have
freed a thousand more if only they knew
they were slaves. Harriet Tubman

All human beings have a worldview—a way of viewing the world, perceiving the world, experiencing the world, understanding the world, making sense of the world. Our worldview can be found in our norms, rituals, customs, laws, traditions, and institutions. It can also be found in our theories, methodologies, technologies, and modes of teaching and learning. Our worldview provides our beliefs, values, fears, hopes, and frames of reference.

Our own worldview also usually reflects the dominant worldview that shapes the social and political organization of our society and the distribution of resources and privileges.

The Nature of Hegemony

> In any society certain positions or perspectives are always domi-
> nant and consequently others are always marginalized and dis-
> enfranchised. The dominant position or perspective is called the
> hegemon. As Trinh T. Minh-ha explains, "Hegemony is estab-
> lished to the extent that the world view of the rulers is also the
> world view of the ruled. It calls attention to the routine structures

1

of everyday thought, down to common sense itself. In dealing with hegemony, we are not only challenging the dominance of Western cultures, but also their identities as unified cultures."

➤ *Hegemony reflects the position or perspective that is (usually) attempting to undermine, marginalize, and disenfranchise other positions or perspectives or systems. It also reflects the position or perspective that has the privileges and resources to undermine, marginalize, and disenfranchise other positions or perspectives or systems.*

➤ *Hegemony is about the ability of a position or perspective to show up with all manner of devices, practices, mechanisms, and structures to impose its position or perspective on others. This includes Communicational practices, Rhetorical practices, Ideological practices, Political practices, Institutional practices, Educational practices, Material practices, and Economic practices.*

Worldviews have ontological, epistemological, and axiological dimensions. The ontological dimension deals with our foundational beliefs about the world and what being human means. Or, simply put, the beliefs that form the foundation of our worldview and give rise to other beliefs. Although no worldview is ever devoid of conflict, tension, and diversity, the Western/European worldview is generally of an ontology that reflects our belief in a world that is of a conflict between positive and negative forces (e.g., order versus chaos, communication versus confusion, meaning versus ambiguity, life versus death, light versus darkness, health versus sickness, knowledge versus ignorance). This belief is prominently seen in the claim by Pythagoras, who is commonly seen as the father of modern mathematics, that *"There is a good principle that created order, light, and man, and an evil principle that created chaos, darkness, and woman."* This belief also forms the foundation of Rene Descartes' philosophy. Descartes lived from 1596 to 1650 is commonly referred to as "The Father of Modern Philosophy." He created analytical geometry and also discovered the laws of refraction and reflection. Descartes believed that human progress and prosperity resided in the mind achieving control and power over the body. Strength is derived by ignoring the supposed weaknesses of the body and relying on the power of the human mind. This is supposedly how we become rational and logical. Descartes' most famous statement—"*I think, therefore I am*"—is about us being defined by our minds. Descartes rejected perception as unreliable, and believed that deductive reasoning (if all birds are blue, the bird outside your window must be blue) was the only reliable method for examining, proving and disproving anything. In other words, Descartes believed that the only reliable method of attaining knowledge is through the mind conquering the body. Our use of standardized tests to supposedly measure the capacity and potentiality of our minds reflects the legacy of Descartes.

The axiological dimension of a worldview deals with how we behave and move in the world, or the politics and ethics of being. Politics is action, and ethics are the frameworks that guide our actions. For example, putting on clothes is politics, and the reason for doing so is ethics. Different worldviews have different beliefs (ontology) that make for different ethics and politics (axiology). Behind putting on clothes is a set of beliefs about what being human means. Such beliefs are absent in cultures where people have no clothes.

The epistemological dimension of a worldview deals with how we perceive and make sense of things. For example, perceiving communication as a process that fundamentally involves removing confusion (noise) is epistemological. This way of perceiving and making sense of communication reflects our foundational belief (axiology) that the world is in a conflict between positive (communication) and negative (confusion) forces. Thus what we believe (ontology) influences how we perceive and make sense of things (epistemology) and in turn influences how we behave and determine what actions are appropriate (axiology). In this case, being ethical involves, amongst other things, communicating in ways that invite neither confusion nor misunderstanding. We describe persons who achieve such accomplishments as being eloquent and coherent.

Besides the different dimensions of a worldview always being in harmony with each other, each dimension also sustains and perpetuates the other dimensions. So again, what we believe will always sustain how we perceive things and in turn shape how we behave. Or, how we behave will reinforce what we believe and how we make sense of things. Every worldview has a certain kind of logic and coherence that is self-reinforcing and self-perpetuating. This logic and coherence is therefore difficult to disrupt. On the other hand, this logic and coherence shapes the limits of our imagination and ultimately what we are capable of sensing, understanding, and experiencing. In this regard, worldviews are powerful things. Our worldviews can enlarge or impede what we can imagine and experience.

This book is about epistemology. That epistemology is about how we perceive and make sense of things means that epistemology is about how we think and what we think about. Epistemology is also about what comes from our thinking, meaning that epistemology is about knowledge, including all the questions that pertain to knowledge.

> ➤ *How do we define knowledge? For example, should knowledge be quantifiable and observable?*
> ➤ *Where does knowledge reside? For example, does knowledge reside inside or outside of us?*
> ➤ *How do we validate knowledge? For example, how does a civilization distinguish true knowledge from false knowledge?*
> ➤ *How do we acquire knowledge? For example, what are the different methodologies different civilizations use to acquire knowledge?*
> ➤ *How do we frame, organize, and share knowledge? For instance, do we use theories, stories, or something else?*
> ➤ *Where do we acquire knowledge? For instance, do we acquire knowledge in classrooms, in temples, in the natural world, or somewhere else?*
> ➤ *What is the purpose of knowledge? For instance, is the purpose of knowledge to help us gain dominion over the world, achieve communion with our gods, or something else?*

Knowledge is about what we recognize, experience, and perceive as real and valuable. We have different knowledges because we recognize, perceive, and experience different things to be real and valuable. The means we use to acquire and organize our knowledge also shape and influence what things we experience, recognize, and perceive as real and valuable.

Because no worldview falls out of the sky, every knowledge system has a historical and geographical context, which means that every system of knowledge can be traced to a certain time and place. Many knowledge systems have origins in conquest—various peoples using a variety of coercive and abusive means to impose their knowledge systems upon others. This kind of conquest commonly defines colonialism and imperialism—movements that aim to coercively impose a foreign worldview on local and indigenous peoples. History presents a narrative of this kind of conquest becoming increasingly efficient and effective.

Different Ways of Achieving Colonialism and Imperialism

- ➤ *Through military force and violence.*
- ➤ *Through religious conversion.*
- ➤ *Through the promotion of literacy and schooling.*
- ➤ *Through foreign aid and philanthropies that often bring the entry of foreign epistemologies, methodologies, and technologies for the supposed sake of promoting progress.*

We can achieve epistemological conquest by military force and violence. Perceive and make sense of the world like us or else face the violent consequences. We can also achieve epistemological conquest by using different kinds of force to erase and discourage indigenous ways of perceiving and making sense of things, beginning with banning or discouraging the languages that local and indigenous peoples use to make sense of things.

The Beginnings of Conquest

Indigenous peoples' diverse languages have developed over many thousands of years in close relationship to their ancestral tribal homelands.

These many hundreds of languages—scholars estimate as many as 300-500 Indigenous languages were once spoken in North America—carry detailed knowledge and observations of the natural world.

While 139 Indigenous languages are miraculously still spoken today in the U.S.—according to UNESCO's Atlas of the World's Languages in Danger—more than 70 are spoken only by the oldest generations of tribal citizens. Some linguists estimate scarcely two dozen Native languages will still be spoken by mid-century; however, a dedicated Native American languages movement has worked for decades to document, publish in, and promote Native language materials and usage among younger generations. This work follows centuries of overt language discrimination and suppression by settlers and religious denominations who actively worked to exterminate Indian languages and cultures beginning in New England the early 1630s with the first grammar schools and "praying towns" providing refuge and "education" to Indian families and students.

Later, federally funded Indian boarding schools were opened by the U.S. War Department's Bureau of Indian Affairs (the Bureau was later moved to the Department of Interior) with an explicit goal to "kill the Indian, save the man," and children from hundreds of tribes were removed from their communities for years at a time to be trained largely as an agricultural, domestic, and industrial labor force. Even into the 1970s and 80s, Native children were often harshly punished or ridiculed for speaking their mother tongues, and as a result, successive generations of tribal peoples did not teach their children their heritage languages in order to shield them from the discrimination and corporal punishment they experienced. Today's Native language teachers and students still face unfair certification and testing practices mandated by more than a decade of prohibitive No Child Left Behind Act regulations, which have continued to undermine Native language classrooms and schools.[1]

---

[1] Excerpted from Our Mother Tongues (2011, October 28). *America's orginal languages.* http://ourmothertongues.org/blog/category/Native-American-Languages-Online.aspx

But using force and violence is by no means the most efficient and effective way of achieving epistemological conquest. History reveals that in the face of such force and violence, native and indigenous people will often resist and devise creative ways to hold onto their local and indigenous knowledge systems. We also achieve epistemological conquest through the promotion of religious missions and religious conversions. To displace a people's conception of God is to displace a people's worldview, as any notion of God contains many foundational beliefs that make for different political and epistemological institutions. Indeed, to take my God as your own is ultimately to take my worldview as your own.

No God But My God

Tactics of Missionaries

The conversion of natives to different forms of Christianity spanned over the course of centuries. The missionaries justified conversion with the notion that they brought the gift of Christianity to the natives, so they were inherently given rights to native land and labor. Some missionaries experienced more success than others (i.e. the Puritans). The success of conversion was often related to the tactics used by the missionaries. Those that exhibited more brutal force, like the Spaniards, found that they were unable to convert large numbers of natives to Christianity. On the other hand those that were less violent towards the natives were able to generate more success.

Spanish Conversion

Franciscan friars were able to develop trusting relationships with tribal chiefs. They served as a link between the chiefs and Spanish officers. Some chiefs came to respect the friars so much that they requested missions to be constructed. These missions were small communities located in the middle of native villages. Their purpose was to provide a place where the natives could be educated in the Catholic teachings as well as to integrate them into European culture.

In addition, Dominican priests also sought to protect the rights of the natives. They often had confrontations with Spanish settlers, as they did not approve of the Europeans' forceful approach to conversion. The European settlers encouraged the Dominican priests to focus on the spiritual aspect regarding the natives, and to let the settlers handle all other matters.

Jesuit Conversion

The Jesuits used a more peaceful approach to converting the natives. Most of the French Jesuits' concentration focused on the Huron tribe in Canada. They attempted to gain converts by living among them and learning about their tribes. At the Sainte-Marie settlement, the missionaries attempted to solidify the relations with the natives by constructing a community where the Europeans and natives lived together. The traditions of each culture were strengthened as they grew to accept each other. Many times the missionaries served merely as the connection between the natives and the fur traders. The natives respected the Jesuits because they attempted to adapt to the local conditions. Although they were not extremely successful with conversion, the Jesuit missionaries were able to maintain peaceful relations with the native tribes.

Puritan Conversion

Many Puritans viewed the Native American tribes as being part of the Lost Tribes of Israel. As such, they felt it was their duty to spread the Christian faith in order to save them. Unlike the Jesuits, the Puritans made no real effort to learn about the native inhabitants. Their relationship consisted of a minimal amount of contact. In effect, the Puritans gave the natives an ultimatum: either convert to Christianity or die from hunger, disease, or violence. In an attempt to help salvage the native population, John Eliot, a well-known Puritan missionary, created praying towns in order to civilize and protect the natives. Indians in these small communities were educated in the teachings of the Christian faith as well as European culture. Mainly only the smaller tribes joined these praying towns in order to survive. By 1674 there were approximately 400 praying Indians and 14 praying towns.

Indian Christian Schools

Schools for native children were created by the missionaries in hopes of spreading Christianity and ultimately transforming them into missionaries as well. One such school was the "Indian Charity School" created by Eleazar Wheelock.

Success of Conversion

Over time, missionaries gradually gained small followings of converts among the native tribes. This conversion included religious as well as cultural change for the natives. As time went on, they began to adopt the dress styles of the Europeans. They strayed from their traditional custom of nakedness in order to cover more flesh and appear more conservative. Samson Occom is a famous example of an Indian convert. He was born into a Mohegan tribe and was greatly influenced by Christian missionaries. He then proceeded to fully adopt the Christian faith and began spreading his newfound beliefs as a missionary. He became a licensed preacher in the Presbyterian church on August 30, 1759.[2]

History reveals that another effective and efficient way to achieve epistemological conquest is by promoting literacy and schooling, especially under the context of merely promoting progress. This kind of conquest can be seen in efforts to make various educational systems global and accessible to all citizens of the world. Left unnoticed are the local and indigenous knowledge systems that these new global educational initiatives will displace and vanquish.

---

[2] Excerpted from *Conversion Tactics* (Gettysburg University). http://www3.gettysburg. edu/~tshannon/hist106web/Indian%20Converts/Conversion%20Tactics.htm

Globalizing Education

I am convinced that digital learning is the most important innovation in education since the printing press. When the class of 2025 arrives on campuses, these technologies will have reshaped the entire concept of college in ways we cannot yet predict. Those transformations may change the whole equation, from access to effectiveness to cost.

To understand the potential, it's important to focus on what digital learning is good for. It is incomparably good at opening possibilities for billions of human beings who have little or no other access to higher learning. The global appetite for advanced learning is enormous.

Yet digital learning also offers surprising advantages even for students with access to the best educational resources. First, digital technologies are remarkably good at teaching content: the basic concepts of circuits and electronics, the principles of chemistry, the evolution of architectural styles.

Digital learning technologies offer a second advantage, which is harder to quantify but is deeply appealing to both students and faculty: flexibility. Just as college traditionally requires four years at the same academic address, traditional courses require large groups of students to regularly gather at the same time and place. By making it possible to break the course content into dozens of small conceptual modules of instruction and testing, digital learning allows students to engage the material anytime, any day, as often as they need to, anywhere in the world.

Digital learning technologies present us with a tremendous opportunity to examine what college is good for, to imagine what colleges might look like in the future and to strive for ways to raise quality and lower costs. To teach what is best learned in person, do we need four years on campus, or could other models be even more effective?

Once we answer these questions, the college experience could look quite different in 10 or 20 years. I expect a range of options, from online credentialing in many technical fields all the way to blended online and residential experiences that could be more stimulating and transformative than any college program in existence now. Higher education will have the tools to engage lifelong learners anywhere, overturning traditional ideas of campus and student body. I believe these experimental years will produce many possibilities, so that future learners will be able to choose what is best for them. If you're wondering how much these options will cost, a better question might be, How much will these options be worth? I strongly believe that by capitalizing on the strengths of online learning, we will make education more accessible, more effective and more affordable for more human beings than ever before.[3]

Another efficient and effective way to achieve epistemological conquest is through the promotion of foreign aid and philanthropy. Foreign aid and philanthropy, besides promoting literacy and schooling, nearly always involve the imposition of foreign methodologies and technologies that achieve epistemological conquest. These foreign epistemologies eventually displace indigenous epistemologies by exposing the inability of indigenous epistemologies to solve local problems, thereby undermining the further practice of indigenous epistemologies. The ability of these foreign epistemologies to seemingly solve local problems also fosters the impression that these epistemologies are inherently superior and thus should be adopted by locals in order for the community to progress. There are also all the resources and promises that come with foreign aid and philanthropy that incentivize the adoption of these foreign methodologies and technologies.

Finally, epistemological conquest is often achieved through seduction—native and indigenous peoples being seduced by the material comforts and technological gains that foreign epistemologies promise.

---

[3] Excerpted from Reif, L. R. (2013, September 26). MIT's President: Better, more affordable colleges start Online. *Time.* http://nation.time.com/2013/09/26/online-learning-will-make-college-cheaper-it-will-also-make-it-better/

In this case, locals become only too eager to adopt these foreign epistemologies. With coercion being unnecessary, this kind of epistemological conquest is arguably the most efficient and effective. But regardless of how a foreign epistemology comes to displace an indigenous epistemology, the entry of a foreign epistemology will soon bring the entry of the ontology and axiology that accompany that epistemology. In other words, the rest of the foreign worldview will eventually show up with all the accompanying social, political, ideological, and epistemological practices and displace the remaining elements of the local and indigenous worldview. This is how worldviews displace other worldviews. This is colonization.

Thus to be colonized is to be:

> *Neutralised*
> *Domesticated*
> *Subdued*
> *Homogenised*
> *Normalised*
> *Subjugated*
> *Terrorised*
> *Traumatized*

Colonization makes the world less diverse, especially less epistemologically diverse. This loss of diversity can be seen in the steady loss of the world's language diversity.

The End Of Language Diversity

Of the estimated 7,000 languages spoken in the world today, linguists say, nearly half are in danger of extinction and are likely to disappear in this century. In fact, they are now falling out of use at a rate of about one every two weeks." K. David Harrison, an assistant professor of linguistics at Swarthmore College in Pennsylvania, said that more than half of the languages have no written form and are "vulnerable to loss and being forgotten." When they disappear, they leave behind no dictionary, no text, no record of the accumulated knowledge and history of a vanished culture. In Australia, nearly all of whose 231 spoken aboriginal tongues are endangered. Many of the 113 languages spoken in the Andes Mountains and Amazon basin are poorly known and are rapidly giving way to Spanish or Portuguese, or in a few cases, to a more-dominant indigenous language.

The dominance of English threatens the survival of the 54 indigenous languages of the Northwest Pacific plateau of North America, a region including British Columbia, Oregon and Washington.

In eastern Siberia, the researchers said, government policies have forced speakers of minority languages to use national and regional languages, such as Russian or Sakha.

Forty American Indian languages are still spoken in Oklahoma, Texas and New Mexico, many of them originally used by indigenous tribes and others introduced by Eastern tribes that were forced to resettle on reservations there, mainly in Oklahoma. Several of the languages are moribund.

Another measure of the threatened decline of many relatively obscure languages, Harrison said, is that speakers and writers of the 83 languages with "global" influence now account for 80 percent of the world population. Most of the thousands of other languages now face extinction at a rate, the researchers said, that exceeds that of birds, mammals, fish or plants.[4]

In fact, every two weeks a language dies and by 2100, more than half of the more than 7,000 languages spoken on Earth are projected to disappear, taking with them a wealth of knowledge about history, culture, the natural environment, and the human brain.

Why Is It Important?

Language defines a culture, through the people who speak it and what it allows speakers to say. Words that describe a particular cultural practice or idea may not translate precisely into another language. Many endangered languages have rich oral cultures with stories,

---

[4] Excerpted from Wilford, J. N. (2007, September 19). Linguists identify endangered language hot spots. *New York Times.* http://www.nytimes.com/2007/09/19/world/asia/19iht-talk.1.7564677.html

songs, and histories passed on to younger generations, but no written forms. With the extinction of a language, an entire culture is lost.

Much of what humans know about nature is encoded only in oral languages. Indigenous groups that have interacted closely with the natural world for thousands of years often have profound insights into local lands, plants, animals, and ecosystems—many still undocumented by science. Studying indigenous languages therefore benefits environmental understanding and conservation efforts.

Studying various languages also increases our understanding of how humans communicate and store knowledge. Every time a language dies, we lose part of the picture of what our brains can do.

Why Do Languages Die Out?

Throughout human history, the languages of powerful groups have spread while the languages of smaller cultures have become extinct. This occurs through official language policies or through the allure that the high prestige of speaking an imperial language can bring. These trends explain, for instance, why more language diversity exists in Bolivia than on the entire European continent, which has a long history of large states and imperial powers.

As big languages spread, children whose parents speak a small language often grow up learning the dominant language. Depending on attitudes toward the ancestral language, those children or their children may never learn the smaller language, or they may forget it as it falls out of use. This has occurred throughout human history, but the rate of language disappearance has accelerated dramatically in recent years.[5]

To colonize is to homogenize, to make others like us in manner, temperament, and worldview. Those doing the colonizing, either deliberately or unintentionally, tend to believe that homogeneity saves us from the strife comes with diversity. It supposedly allows a society to function smoothly, efficiently, and productively. The relation between ontology and axiology emerges again—believing that the world is of a

---

[5] Excerpted from *Disappearing Languages* http://www.todaytranslations.com/blog/disappearing-languages/

conflict between homogeneity and diversity makes for a suspicion of diversity. That is, diversity emerges as a threat to all that is good and decent.

However, our erosion of human diversity is contrary to the world's natural order and rhythm, which is to promote diversity. As Nobel Laureate Freeman Dyson (2000) observes, *"I do not claim any ability to read God's mind. I am sure of only one thing. When we look at the glory of stars and galaxies in the sky and the glory of forests and flowers in the living world around us, it is evident that God loves diversity. Perhaps the universe is constructed according to a principle of maximum diversity. The principle of maximum diversity says that the laws of nature, and the initial conditions at the beginning of time, are such as to make the universe as interesting as possible."*[6] Indeed, probably the most self-evident truth is that life flourishes through the promotion of diversity. Nevertheless, when a worldview is dominant the epistemological consequences are profound.

> ➢ *It shapes our understanding of everything.*
> ➢ *It dictates what we know to be true and real.*
> ➢ *It shapes how a people will experience the world.*
> ➢ *It silences, erases, marginalizes, and delegitimizes the people who represent Other worldviews.*
> ➢ *It fosters the ideals of progress, success, and civility for all peoples.*
> ➢ *It silences, erases, marginalizes, and delegitimizes other worldviews.*

Worldviews are inherently hostile to each other. Different world-views mean different values, beliefs, fears, truths, norms, and so forth. Famous examples of persons being persecuted for challenging a dominant worldview include Galileo, Moses, Muhammad, and Jesus Christ. The reason for the hostility is because emerging worldviews and the persons who represent those worldviews challenge the legitimacy and authority of the dominant worldview, as well as the privileges that

---

[6] Dyson, F. (2000, May 16). Progress in religion. *Edge.* http://www.edge.org/documents/archive/edge68.html

come with being of the dominant worldview. However, as much as the differences between worldviews are often difficult to reconcile, this in no way means that strife and violence are inevitable. It also in no way means reconciling the differences between worldviews is necessary for peace and prosperity. We can have diversity (and even conflict) without strife and violence as both have origins in something other than our diversity. To believe that our differences make for strife and violence is to believe that the Holocaust was about Jews being different, or that slavery and Jim Crow was about African-Americans being different.

In this book I use *communication studies* as a case study to show the workings of an epistemology and also how this epistemology achieves and sustains hegemony (domination). I am specifically interested in showcasing how an epistemology comes to control how we perceive and make sense of things (in this case the theorizing and teaching of communication), and the consequences that come from this hegemony, such as the loss of other ways of understanding, theorizing, and teaching communication that can potentially expand our sense of what the world can become. I am interested in communication studies as a new kind of colonialism that insidiously perpetuates a Western/European worldview. Like all the other sciences and disciplines (e.g., psychology, sociology, biology) that form the foundation of Western/European civilization, communication studies is simply assumed to be a science devoid of history and ideology.

But this is an illusion. In this book I highlight the history and ideology that frames communication studies and show how both work to perpetuate a certain understanding of communication that is in harmony with a Western/European worldview. Nothing is inherently wrong with a worldview cultivating harmony. My point is that the epistemology that rules communication studies impoverishes our understanding of communication and ultimately the human experience. I am interested in revealing the workings of this epistemology, as well as the workings of this epistemology as a hegemon.

Two

On Being Epistemologically Colonized

> ➤ Epistemological conquest is about our imposing our view of the world on others by way of imposing how we perceive and make sense of the world on others. It is making people think like how we think. By being able to impose how we perceive and make sense of the world on others we also change what these people view as good, decent, and beautiful. Now we define and dictate what is good, decent, and beautiful.

Speak English

The 1868 Indian Peace Commission made a number of recommendations on how to subjugate Western tribes. "In the difference of language today lies two-thirds of our trouble.... Schools should be established which children would be required to attend; their barbarous dialects would be blotted out and the English language substituted. ... Through sameness of language is produced sameness of sentiment, and thought; customs and habits are moulded and assimilated in the same way" Thus was born the United States Bureau of Indian Affairs school system with the primary mission of using coercion to promote English instruction and assimilation. By 1886 federal Indian education funds were reserved exclusively for English-language instruction.

The U.S. government also eventually imposed English as the language of instruction in Hawaii, the Philippines, and Puerto Rico.[7]

➤ Epistemological conquest is also about claiming the power to determine who/what should live and who/what should die.

Assimilation Now

On a more philosophical level, do we want to keep people in a "cultural museum," a time warp as it were? Putting aside the practical questions of how this would be accomplished, is it morally the right thing to do? This is a question of values and some of my anthropologist colleagues would say yes. But the morality of this question has to be considered in the light of our own cultural origins. Once upon a time, the ancestors of each and every one of us lived in a premodern culture. Those cultural origins have now been completely erased from our collective memory. Do any of us regret the loss of this memory? Would any of us prefer to return to our ancestral condition, rather than to live in the modern world? Few, if any, would say yes. To live in isolation is to live a short, hard life in the absence of modern medicine and in complete ignorance of history, geography, science, and art.

To my admittedly biased way of thinking, the modern world offers a vastly richer existence—intellectually, culturally, physically. Not only do we live nearly twice as long on average, but we are able to travel, to experience the accomplishments of a cultural history that goes back three thousand years, and to savor the best creations of a highly diverse global cuisine. Recently contacted people I've met in both New Guinea and the Amazon were grateful for contact. For the first time, they were able to move freely without the burden of anxiety that comes from living in a state of hostility with neighbors or the outside world. Really, it's no contest, and many of the Amazonians

---

[7] Language Policy Task Force. (1978). Language policy and the Puerto Rican community. *Bilingual Review, 5*, 1-39. Leibowitz, A. (1969). English literacy: Legal sanction for discrimination. *Notre Dame Lawyer, 45*, 7-67.

I know, especially of the younger generation, are eager to immerse themselves in Western society.

The question is, how to make the leap? The cultural gulf is both wide and deep and there is no easy way to jump over it. . . . [How can we] assist isolated people negotiate the leap into modern life. A native Amazonian does not know how to function in contemporary society. He or she speaks an unwritten language and is possessed of jungle skills that are of little value in the money economy. Add to these handicaps the almost universal tendency of frontier societies to exploit and discriminate against the members of less acculturated ethnic groups, and the barriers are almost insurmountable. Social ostracism, demoralization, and alcoholism comprise the barren netherworld between cultural states. . . .

[I]n my view, assimilation offers the only moral and permanent option. The cultural gap can be bridged, but only by education. Yet the educational services provided to unacculturated natives are usually abysmal. Here might be the starting point for a fourth-generation policy that would break new ground while benefiting from insights gained through the experiences of thousands of Amazonians who paid for the mistakes of the past with their lives.[8]

> ➤ Finally, epistemological conquest is having others view our theories, methodologies, and pedagogies as devoid of ideology and politics thereby devoid of beliefs, fears, values, and hopes. So science becomes merely a means for finding the *Truth* and presumably has nothing to do with politics and ideology. However, because nothing falls out of the sky, science too is a human creation. It is shaped by politics and ideology and serves the interests of a certain kind of politics and ideology. This reality is most evident in science's hostility to new and novel

---

[8] John Terborgh (Research Professor in the Nicholas School of the Environment and Earth Sciences at Duke and Director of its Center for Tropical Conservation, April 5, 2012, *The New York Review of Books*).

questions. According to Thomas Kuhn, *"Normal science, the activity in which most scientists inevitably spend almost all their time, is predicted on the assumption that the scientific community knows what the world is like. Much of the success of the enterprise derives from the community's willingness to defend that assumption, if necessary at considerable cost. Normal science, for example, often suppresses fundamental novelties because they are necessarily subversive of its basic commitments"* (p. 5.)

The Nature Of Science

Science reflects the Western/European worldview's belief that progress comes from the building of supposedly rigorous institutional practices. Presumably, only such practices will make for findings that are valuable and reliable. If there is a problem with the findings that science predicts, the fault is presumably with the process. However, the processes that are of science only make for a certain kind of findings, those that will pose no threat to the status quo. As Thomas Kuhn (1996) explains, *"No part of the aim of normal science is to call forth new sorts of phenomena; indeed those that will not fit the box are often not seen at all. Nor do scientists normally aim to invent new theories, and they are often intolerant of those invented by others. Instead, normal-scientific research is directed to the articulation of those phenomena and theories that the paradigm already supplies"* (p. 24). In fact, *"A paradigm can, for that matter, even insulate the community from those socially important problems that are not reducible to the puzzle form, because they cannot be stated in terms of the conceptual and instrumental tools the paradigm supplies. Such problems can be a distraction . . . . One of the reasons why normal science seems to progress so rapidly is that its practitioners concentrate on problems that only their own lack of ingenuity should keep them from solving"* (p. 37).[9] Consequently, no paper that poses a threat to anything has ever been published in a supposedly prestigious scholarly communication journal. In keeping us bound to a certain set of

---

[9] Kuhn, T. S. (1996). *The structure of scientific revolutions*. Chicago: University of Chicago Press.

institutional practices that demand conformity in order to maintain supposed standards of scholarly excellence, science neutralizes possible threats to the status quo by blocking the rise of any knowledge that falls outside the bounds of science. In lacking the seal of science, such knowledge, and the persons who represent that knowledge, will never be seen as credible.

Three

On the Consequences of Being Epistemologically Colonized

An analogy of colonization can be found in the creating and maintaining of lawns and gardens. Both represent our imposing our worldview through force and violence on a certain set of species. Before our coming there was already a thriving ecology with a diversity of grass, plants, trees, and other species in that space where we now want our perfectly manicured lawns and gardens. However, the species that were already there violated our conception of beauty. So through our methodologies and technologies, those local and indigenous species were forcibly removed and replaced with species that conformed to our conception of beauty. In many cases these new species were of our making, created by us using our knowledge of grass and plants to meet our own needs, desires, and standards of beauty.

But because these new species are foreign to this new place, and with many local and indigenous species (like dandelions) often refusing to be easily displaced and vanquished, extraordinary measures—as in violence—become increasingly necessary for the conquest to be successful. A lot of highly dangerous herbicides and pesticides must increasingly be used to oppressively subdue the local and indigenous species, which eventually of course come to be seen as "weeds" that threaten the health and prosperity of our perfect lawns and gardens. The ugly names given to local and indigenous species (e.g., crabgrass) also reinforce the view that these species are a menace that must be neutralized. By our own thinking and reasoning, force and violence become legitimate means of dealing with these local and indigenous species that refuse to submit to our will. Such species always emerge as threats to us, and are thereby deserving of being vanquished.

Advertisement For Lawn Care Services

Pests and weeds can be the bane of any lawn. They take over the grass and leave your lawn looking dull and lifeless. Therefore, if you want a vibrant and healthy lawn, you will need to take some serious action. Pest and weed control for lawns is a great way to put life back into your yard and restore your lawn to a healthy and lush state.

At Metro Lawn Sprinklers and Landscapes, we provide quality pest and weed control for lawns. Our services are available for both commercial as well as residential clients located throughout the St. Peters and St. Louis areas. Call us today to request a quote on pest and weed control for lawns or to find out about our other lawn maintenance services that we offer.

Benefits of Our Pest and Weed Control for Lawns

Proper pest and weed control for lawns and other turf areas can ensure that the grass stays healthy and looking its best any time of the year. It will help prevent damage from insect infestations and can prevent the growth and spread of certain funguses and weeds. Therefore, pest and weed control for lawns is one of the most important lawn maintenance services.

Here are some of the main reasons why you should take advantage of our pest and weed control services:

- *Achieve Better Looking Yards: Any lawn that has been eaten away by pests or dominated by weeds looks dull and bleak. With our pest and weed control for lawns, your yard will look better in just a few short weeks. Pesticides and herbicides destroy the harmful pests and weeds, letting your grass grow freely.*

- *Promote Healthier Grass: Grass that is under constant attack by weeds and pests does not just look dull, it is unhealthy too. When you use pest and weed control for lawns, you can restore life back into your grass. Without the constant dominance of weeds, your grass will develop stronger roots and look naturally more vibrant over time.*
- *Protect the Environment: Certain pests and weeds can be detrimental to the natural environment. Controlling these harmful weeds and pests can be better for the natural surroundings. Additionally, all the herbicides and pesticides we use are completely safe and will not damage the environment.*[10]

But as with any kind of colonialism, our quest for perfect lawns and gardens come with a negative set of consequences that eventually fall back on us and those who are the subject of our colonizing.

The Fallout

➤ Creating and maintaining perfect lawns and gardens require the use of machines that burn enormous amounts fossil fuels. Thus maintaining these lawns and gardens contribute to global warming.

Burn Baby Burn

Lush green lawns may not be as good for the environment as you might think.

A new study suggests that, in certain parts of the country, total emissions would actually be lower if there weren't any lawns.

Previous studies have demonstrated that lawns comprised of turfgrass can potentially function as carbon sinks since they help remove

---

[10] Metro Lawn Sprinklers and Landscapes http://www.metrolawnsprinkler.com/pest-and-weed-control.html

*carbon dioxide from the atmosphere. But the maintenance of lawns —
fertilizer production, mowing, leaf blowing and other lawn management practices — may generate greenhouse gas emissions that ultimately are similar to or greater than the carbon they end up storing,
according to the study.*

*"Lawns look great — they're nice and green and healthy, and they're
photosynthesizing a lot of organic carbon," said researcher Amy
Townsend-Small, who co-authored the study. "But the carbon-stor-
ing benefits of lawns are counteracted by fuel consumption."*

*To reach their conclusion, the researchers sampled grass from four
parks around Irvine, Calif. that contained either ornamental lawn turf
or athletic field turf, which tended to be more trampled and required
replanting and frequent aeration. Samples were taken from the soil
and air above the turf, and analyzed to measure carbon sequestration
and nitrous oxide emissions. The investigators then compared that
data to the amount of carbon dioxide emissions that resulted from
maintaining the turf, which included fuel consumption, irrigation and
fertilizer production.*

The results, detailed in the forthcoming issue of the journal
Geophysical Research Letters, *showed that nitrous oxide emissions
from lawns were comparable to those found in agricultural farms,
which are considered among the largest emitters of nitrous oxide
globally. In ornamental lawns, nitrous oxide emissions from fertiliza-
tion offset just 10 percent to 30 percent of the carbon that was seques-
tered. But day-to-day management required fossil fuel consumption
that released as much or more carbon dioxide than the plots could
take up.*[11]

---

[11] Excerpted from "Lawns May Contribute To Global Warming." (2010, January 21).
Live Science. http://www.livescience.com/8031-lawns-contribute-global-warming.
html

> ➤ Creating and maintaining perfect lawns and gardens contribute to the depletion of natural resources.

Water Now

LOS ANGELES — This is how officials here feel about grass these days: since 2009, the city has paid $1.4 million to homeowners willing to rip out their front lawns and plant less thirsty landscaping.

At least the lawns are still legal here. Grass front yards are banned at new developments in Las Vegas, where even the grass medians on the Strip have been replaced with synthetic turf.

In Austin, Tex., lawns are allowed; watering them, however, is not — at least not before sunset. Police units cruise through middle-class neighborhoods hunting for sprinklers running in daylight and issuing $475 fines to their owners.

Worried about dwindling water supplies, communities across the drought-stricken Southwest have begun waging war on a symbol of suburban living: the lush, green grass of front lawns.

In hopes of enticing, or forcing, residents to abandon the scent of freshly cut grass, cities in this parched region have offered homeowners ever-increasing amounts to replace their lawns with drought-resistant plants; those who keep their grass face tough watering restrictions and fines for leaky sprinklers.

These efforts are drastically reshaping the landscape, with cactuses and succulents taking over where green grass once reigned.

"The era of the lawn in the West is over," said Paul Robbins, the director of the Nelson Institute for Environmental Studies at the University of Wisconsin. "The water limits are insurmountable, unless the Scotts

Company develops a genetically modified grass that requires almost no water. And I'm sure it's keeping them up at night."

In Mesa, Ariz., the city has paid to turn nearly 250,000 square feet of residential lawn into desertscape.

More than one million square feet of grass has been moved from Los Angeles residences since the rebate program began here in 2009. New parks provide only token patches of grass, surrounded by native plants. Outside City Hall, what was once a grassy park has been transformed into a garden of succulents.

The first five months of this year were the driest on record in California, with reservoirs in the state at 20 percent below normal levels. The lawn rebate program here will save approximately 47 million gallons of water each year, according to the Los Angeles Department of Water and power.

Las Vegas presents a model of how quickly the landscape can change when a city moves aggressively. In 2003, after a drought wiped out the city's water resources, the Las Vegas Valley Water District offered what officials believe was the first turf removal rebate program in the country.

Since then, the water district has paid out nearly $200 million to remove 165.6 million square feet of grass from residences and businesses.[12]

> ➤ Creating and maintaining perfect lawns and gardens require the use of highly dangerous chemicals which eventually enter the water supply, food chain, and our own bodies.

[12] Excerpted from Lovett, I. (2013, August 11). Arid Southwest Cities' Plea: Lose the Lawn. *New York Times*. http://www.nytimes.com/2013/08/12/us/to-save-water-parched-southwest-cities-ask-homeowners-to-lose-their-lawns. html?_r=2&&pagewanted=print

The Price of Beauty

Turfgrasses have a seasonal cycle: they grow quickly when conditions are favorable—for cool-weather species like Kentucky bluegrass, this is in spring, while for warm-weather species like Bermuda grass it's in summer—and then they slow down. During the slow phase, the grass becomes dull-colored or, if the weather is dry, yellow or brown. In 1909, a German chemist named Fritz Haber figured out how to synthesize ammonia. One use for what became known as the Haber-Bosch process was to manufacture explosives—the process was perfected just in time for the First World War—and a second was to produce synthetic fertilizer. It was observed that repeated applications of synthetic fertilizer could counteract turfgrasses' seasonal cycle by, in effect, tricking the plants into putting out new growth. Sensing a potential bonanza, lawn-care companies began marketing the idea of an ever-green green. The Scotts Company recommended that customers apply its fertilizer, Turf Builder, no fewer than five times a year.

With the advent of herbicides, in the nineteen-forties, still tighter control became possible. As long as a hand trowel was the only option, weeding a lawn had been considered more or less hopeless, and most guides advised against even trying. The new herbicides allowed gardeners to kill off plants that they didn't care for with a single spraying.

One of the most popular herbicides was—and continues to be—2,4-dichlorophenoxyacetic acid, or 2,4-D, as it is commonly known, a major ingredient in Agent Orange. Regrettably, 2,4-D killed not only dandelions but also plants that were beneficial to lawns, like nitrogen-fixing clover. To cover up this loss, any plant that the chemical eradicated was redefined as an enemy. "Once considered the ultimate in fine turf, a clover lawn is looked upon today by most authorities as not much better than a weed patch" is how one guidebook explained the change.

The greener, purer lawns that the chemical treatments made possible were, as monocultures, more vulnerable to pests, and when grubs attacked the resulting brown spot showed up like lipstick on a collar. The answer to this chemically induced problem was to apply more chemicals. As Paul Robbins reports in "Lawn People" (2007), the first pesticide popularly spread on lawns was lead arsenate, which tended to leave behind both lead and arsenic contamination. Next in line were DDT and chlordane. Once they were shown to be toxic, pesticides like diazinon and chlorpyrifos—both of which affect the nervous system—took their place. Diazinon and chlorpyrifos, too, were eventually revealed to be hazardous. (Diazinon came under scrutiny after birds started dropping dead around a recently sprayed golf course.) The insecticide carbaryl, which is marketed under the trade name Sevin, is still broadly applied to lawns. A likely human carcinogen, it has been shown to cause developmental damage in lab animals, and is toxic to—among many other organisms—tadpoles, salamanders, and honeybees. In "American Green" (2006), Ted Steinberg, a professor of history at Case Western Reserve University, compares the lawn to "a nationwide chemical experiment with homeowners as the guinea pigs."

Meanwhile, the risks of the chemical lawn are not confined to the people who own the lawns, or to the creatures that try to live in them. Rain and irrigation carry synthetic fertilizers into streams and lakes, where the excess nutrients contribute to algae blooms that, in turn, produce aquatic "dead zones." Manhattanites may not keep lawns, but they drink the chemicals that run off them. A 2002 report found traces of thirty-seven pesticides in streams feeding into the Croton River Watershed. A few years ago, Toronto banned the use of virtually all lawn pesticides and herbicides, including 2,4-D and carbaryl, on the ground that they pose a health risk, especially to children.[13]

---

[13] Excerpted from Kolbert, E. (2008, July 21). Turf war. *New Yorker*. http://www.newyorker.com/arts/critics/books/2008/07/21/080721crbo_books_kolbert?printable=true&currentPage=all

> ➤ Creating and maintaining perfect lawns and gardens contribute to the loss of ecological diversity.

Losing Our Diversity

The conventional approach of landscaping with turf and ornamentals impacts biodiversity in two ways: 1) it limits the diversity of native species in areas dominated by turf and ornamentals, and 2) it can impact surrounding natural environments, altering habitats in ways that exclude native plants and animals. Simply put, landscapes dominated by turfgrass and non-native ornamental plants create an artificial environment that offers very little opportunity for most native species to thrive. A monoculture of turfgrass infused with non-native ornamentals excludes native plants and provides little to no habitat for most wildlife. Think about the vast amount of land devoted to turf, both for growing the sod and the amount of sod that occurs on the landscape as urban lawns. One estimate indicates that four million acres of managed turfgrass occurs in Florida, with 75 percent of these as residential lawns. Such acreage limits the amount of natural habitat, thus decreasing urban habitat diversity and ultimately native species diversity.

With animals, studies show that many wildlife species are not found or are in low abundance in turfgrass/non-native, dominated habitats, particularly our most sensitive and endemic species. Bird species that were normally found in more natural areas gradually drop out along a gradient of urbanization. Native insect and spider diversity declines in urban areas dominated by turf. As areas become more urban, native plant species disappear and non-natives increase in number. In general, biodiversity indices decrease as one goes towards urban centers.

However, biodiversity measures improve with the use of native plants. For example, native urban bird diversity increases with native vegetation, more native plants serve as host plants for butterfly larvae; and native bee diversity increases with the occurrence of native plants. Although some exotic plants, particularly trees and shrubs, can provide food and shelter for some animals, it is fair to say that the negatives of a landscape dominated by non-native plants far outweigh the positives for wildlife. First, the exclusive use of non-native plants would ultimately decrease native plant diversity because of the simple fact that native plants are absent from the area. Second, native animal diversity, in general, is correlated to native vegetation diversity. Overall, the diversity of native plants improves urban biodiversity by simultaneously creating wildlife habitat and increasing the presence of native plants.

Both within and beyond city boundaries, the maintenance of lawns and exotic plants with an array of insecticides, fertilizers, and herbicides can also impact biodiversity. With insecticides and herbicides, most people use these chemicals to keep other plants out and to keep turf and ornamentals healthy and alive. The end result is usually the eradication of native plants and insects. For example, many insecticides are not specific to the pest insect and kill many of our native pollinators such as bees, beetles, wasps, and butterflies. Applying herbicides to get rid of "weeds" reduces biodiversity simply because the weeds can be native plants embedded within landscaped and turf areas. Roundup, and its active ingredient isopropylamine, was found to be toxic to native freshwater mussels and lethal to both aquatic and terrestrial amphibians. The end result is a net native biodiversity loss as local native plants and animals can be eradicated from a yard or neighborhood, a nearby water body, and even surrounding natural habitat.

How do fertilizers impact biodiversity? Excess fertilizers (e.g., phosphate and nitrate that is not taken up by yard plants) end up in local wetlands and waterbodies when nutrients run off the landscape after a storm event. Rivers, streams, and lakes that have high levels of nitrates and phosphates cause algal blooms, fish kills, and the growth of invasive exotic plants.

Biodiversity loss can even affect important ecosystem services, such as removal of carbon dioxide (CO_2) and pollination services. More biodiverse ecosystems can uptake more CO_2, a greenhouse gas, than ecosystems with less species diversity.[14]

> Lawns and manicured gardens often surround homes and subdivisions built on prime farmland.

The Reckoning

Earth is rapidly headed toward a catastrophic breakdown if humans don't get their act together, according to an international group of scientists.

Writing in the journal Nature, the researchers warn that the world is headed toward a tipping point marked by extinctions and unpredictable changes on a scale not seen since the glaciers retreated 12,000 years ago.

"There is a very high possibility that by the end of the century, the Earth is going to be a very different place," study researcher Anthony Barnosky told LiveScience. Barnosky, a professor of integrative biology from the University of California, Berkeley, joined a group of 17 other scientists to warn that this new planet might not be a pleasant place to live.

"You can envision these state changes as a fast period of adjustment where we get pushed through the eye of the needle," Barnosky said. "As we're going through the eye of the needle, that's when we see political strife, economic strife, war and famine."

---

[14] Excerpted from Hostetler, M. E., & Main, M. B. *Native Landscaping vs. Exotic Landscaping: What Should We Recommend?* http://www.wec.ufl.edu/extension/gc/harmony/landscaping/nativeandexotic.htm

Barnosky and his colleagues reviewed research on climate change, ecology and Earth's tipping points that break the camel's back, so to speak. At certain thresholds, putting more pressure on the environment leads to a point of no return, Barnosky said. Suddenly, the planet responds in unpredictable ways, triggering major global transitions.

The most recent example of one of these transitions is the end of the last glacial period. Within not much more than 3,000 years, the Earth went from being 30 percent covered in ice to its present, nearly ice-free condition. Most extinctions and ecological changes (goodbye, woolly mammoths) occurred in just 1,600 years. Earth's biodiversity still has not recovered to what it was.

Today, Barnosky said, humans are causing changes even faster than the natural ones that pushed back the glaciers — and the changes are bigger. Driven by a 35 percent increase in atmospheric carbon dioxide since the start of the Industrial Revolution, global temperatures are rising faster than they did back then, Barnosky said. Likewise, humans have completely transformed 43 percent of Earth's land surface for cities and agriculture, compared with the 30 percent land surface transition that occurred at the end of the last glacial period. Meanwhile, the human population has exploded, putting ever more pressure on existing resources.

"Every change we look at that we have accomplished in the past couple of centuries is actually more than what preceded one of these major state changes in the past," Barnosky said.

The results are difficult to predict, because tipping points, by their definition, take the planet into uncharted territory. Based on past transitions, Barnosky and his colleagues predict a major loss of species (during the end of the last glacial period, half of the large-bodied mammal species in the world disappeared), as well as changes in the makeup of species in various communities on the local level.

Meanwhile, humans may well be knotting our own noose as we burn through Earth's resources.

"These ecological systems actually give us our life support, our crops, our fisheries, clean water," Barnosky said. As resources shift from one nation to another, political instability can easily follow.

Pulling back from the ledge will require international cooperation, Barnosky said. Under business-as-usual conditions, humankind will be using 50 percent of the land surface on the planet by 2025. It seems unavoidable that the human population will reach 9 billion by 2050, so we'll have to become more efficient to sustain ourselves, he said. That means more efficient energy use and energy production, a greater focus on renewable resources, and a need to save species and habitat today for future generations.

"My bottom line is that I want the world in 50 to 100 years to be at least as good as it is now for my children and their children, and I think most people would say the same," Barnosky said. "We're at a cross-roads where if we choose to do nothing we really do face these tipping points and a less-good future for our immediate descendents."[15]

Using lawns as an analogy of colonialism is to understand that colonialism is a destructive process for those doing the colonizing and those who are subject to the colonizing. Using lawns as an analogy is also to understand that colonialism is about the ability of a worldview to show up with the power and resources to impose its vision of the world on others. Indeed, this analogy allows us to understand that there is nothing natural and ecological about colonization. It will always be destructive, either by destroying human diversity or simply by producing a set of destructive effects that fall back on all of us. Also, because the order that colonialism seeks to impose is both unnatural and unecological,

---

[15] Excerpted from Pappas, S. (2012, June 7). Earth Tipping Point Study In Nature Journal Predicts Disturbing And Unpredictable Changes. *Huffington Post.* http://www.huffingtonpost.com/2012/06/07/earth-tipping-point-study_n_1577835.html

this order will always need extraordinary measures in order to remain in place. We will always have to apply new treatments to subdue and neutralize the local and indigenous peoples. Thus to use lawns as an analogy is to understand that many local and indigenous peoples will always resist colonialism. There will always be struggle and resistance.

Using lawns as an analogy for colonization is to also understand how racism is bound up with colonization. Colonization is about the imposition of an order that reflects a certain people's conception of beauty, civility, decency, and goodness at the cost of devaluing and even vanquishing other people's conceptions of these notions. It is about believing that our conceptions are superior and making others believe so as well. Colonization is also about commanding the position to judge the worth of Other peoples' conceptions, including defining and setting the standards by which those conceptions will be judged. That is, colonization is about owning and commanding the power to judge who and what should live. All of this can be put in the form of a question: *How do we acquire the right to judge a species—such as dandelions—to be ugly, and to rule that this species must die?* This is colonization. But this is also racism—being able to dictate and declare which species are good and beautiful, and being able to torment and even vanquish those judged to be bad and ugly. Racism is also about being able to remain oblivious to the fact that our standards of beauty, decency, civility, and goodness are of our making, for our own purposes. Such are the privileges that colonization affords. There will be no challenging of our arbitrary standards. Nor will there be any challenging of the power we assume to determine who and what will either live or die.

Four

The Psychology of Being Colonized

What becomes of our psychology in the face of the belief that our worldview is inferior? Indeed, there are many effects that come with being colonized—that is, being neutralized, domesticated, subdued, homogenized, normalized, subjugated, terrorized, and traumatized. Adopting the worldview of another people involves believing that our own worldview, including all the beliefs, values, practices, and behaviors that are of our worldview, is inferior. Internalizing this belief eventually makes for a deep suspicion and even hostility to our own worldview, often seen in our own attempts to disown and discredit anything that is of our worldview and, to use Franz Fanon's words, annihilate our own presence.

Language & Colonialism

Recently, the Oakland School District of California passed a resolution granting pedagogical legitimacy to a language commonly referred to as Black English or Ebonics. There was almost unanimous protest against the resolution. Prominent members of the Black community accused the Oakland School District of being ignorant, irresponsible, and incompetent.

> *I understand the attempt to reach out to these children, but this is an unacceptable surrender, border-lining on disgrace. It's teaching down to our children and it must never happen. I appeal to that board to please reverse that decision because they're becoming really, unfortunately, the laughingstock of the nation.*
> Rev. Jesse Jackson, Founder & President Rainbow Coalition

> *Ebonics . . . is a cruel joke. . . . There is, within the larger African American community, and in other communities, various dialects. They're not languages, they are dialects . . . We have to find ways to bridge out of that into proper English.*
> Kweisi Mfume, President, NAACP

> *I think it's tragic.*
> Ward Connerly, Regent, University of California

> *Ebonics is not a foreign or distinct language. It should neither be taught in the classroom, nor accommodated there.*
> Sen. Ray Haynes, Riverside

> *I be thinking that [Ebonics] be real ignorant.*
> Spike Lee

> *Ignoromics.*
> Bill Cosby

> *Quite frankly, the Oakland strategy seems to be pedagogy run amok. . . . We in this country need to catch ourselves . . . . Neither our nation, nor our nation of children, has the time for this [foolishness].*

A.J. Verdelle, Bunting Institute,
Harvard University

*If Oakland's School Board accomplished nothing else, it gave people . . .
something to laugh at over the holidays.*
Ellis Cose, Editor-at-Large, Newsweek

*I'm incensed [about the resolution]. . . the very idea that African
American language is a separate language can be very threatening,
because it can encourage young men and women not to learn standard English.*

*I can't believe that we are talking about Ebonics as if it really is a
condition other than ignorance. If I was an English teacher, I would
be up in arms that someone told me I had to translate slang so I could
teach somebody English.*
Maya Angelou, Poet

*I consider this institutionalized dysfunction . . . . Our aspiration
has to be excellence in English. I would not vote to expose our children under the guise that you are imparting something of value.
I do not go along. . . . I understand and applaud cultural and linguistic diversity, but I reject all arguments that carry political cor-
rectness to the extreme of promoting anything other than English
as our official language. . . . The only place for Ebonics is in the
streets. We don't need it in the classroom; we need to rescue kids
from Ebonics.*
Eldridge Cleaver, Founding Member & Minister of Information,
Black Panther Party

*The school board . . . blundered badly . . . when it declared that black
slang is a distinct language that warrants a place of respect in the
classroom. . . . the new policy will . . . stigmatize African-American
children.*
The New York Times, Editorial

Last week's unanimous vote by Oakland's school board resurrected the ludicrous idea that a vernacular form of English—in this case, what is called black English or Ebonics—should be recognized as a primary language. . . . But, in the desire to be culturally sensitive, let's not lose sight of one key goal: mastery of standard English. That is the single best route to decent jobs and higher education in this country for students of all backgrounds. Anything that distracts schools and students away from that path is a foolish diversion.
The Seattle Times, Editorial

Missed in the controversy and the media firestorm over the resolution by the Oakland School Board was the support of linguists for the decision and for Ebonics as a legitimate language. Thus unnoticed was the statement quickly put out by *The Linguistic Society of America* that said, in part, *"In fact, all human linguistic systems—spoken, signed, and written—are fundamentally regular. . . . [T]he Oakland School Board's decision to recognize the vernacular of African American students in teaching them Standard English is linguistically and pedagogically sound."* Also unnoticed were the statements by many of the most accomplished linguists in the world.

People used to believe that African American English was illogical, poorly constructed and inadequate for any cognitive or linguistic growth. . . . But while it is certainly different from Standard English, it is not inferior.
John R. Rickford, Linguist,
Department of Linguistics, Stanford University

Many prescriptive rules of grammar are just plain dumb and should be deleted from the usage handbooks. And most of standard English is just that, standard, in the same sense that certain units of currency or household voltages are said to be standard. It is just common sense that people should be given every encouragement and opportunity to learn the dialect that has become standard in their society and to employ it in many formal settings. But there is no

need to use terms like "bad grammar," "fractured syntax," and incorrect usage" when referring to rural and black dialects. . . . using terms like "bad grammar" for "nonstandard" is both insulting and scientifically inaccurate.
Steven Pinker, Harvard University

What makes standard English standard is a matter of social attitudes and the political power of those who speak the standard dialect. . . . Because standard English speakers control education, commerce, government, and other powerful institutions, the standard dialect is firmly associated with public life.
Carolyn Temple Adger,
Center for Applied Linguistics

The Ebonics controversy is, finally and most importantly, a fight . . . about language . . . as an instrument of influence and social control. . . . who controls language . . . [and] the words that can be used for public discourse . . . determines . . . what can and should be listened to and taken seriously.
Robin Lakoff, Professor of Linguistics,
University of California, Berkeley

Negative reactions against Ebonics and the Oakland School Board . . . reflect racist assumptions about the language and educational needs of Black working-class and un-working-class people . . . . Assault on the language of African America is a way of reinscribing the subordination and powerlessness of Black working-class people in this country.
Geneva Smitherman, University Distinguished Professor of English, Michigan State University

This particular issue is just shot through with politics. By and large, linguists are not going to get into arguments about what's a language, what's not a language. Language is not a technical term. It is a political and ideological term.

Wayne O'Neil, Chairman of the Linguistics and Philosophy Department at the Massachusetts Institute of Technology

This African American Vernacular English shares most of its grammar and vocabulary with other dialects of English. But it is distinct in many ways, and it is more different from standard English than any other dialect spoken in continental North America. It is not simply slang, or grammatical mistakes, but a well-formed set of rules of pronunciation and grammar that is capable of conveying complex logic and reasoning.
William Labov, Professor of Linguistics, University of Pennsylvania

Language is culture. It is very important that a child's language and a child's culture be recognized and valued.
Noma Anderson, Chairperson, Department of Communications Sciences and Disorders, Howard University

I will submit that one of the reasons that it [Ebonics] is a problem, if you will—a controversy—is that you cannot divorce language from its speakers. And if you have a people who have been disenfranchised, are neglected, are rejected, it is very difficult for the society at large to elevate their language. And, thus, when you start to try to make a case with legitimizing Ebonics. . . you, in effect, are talking about legitimizing a group of people. You're talking about bringing them to a status comparable to society at large. And that's always a difficult proposition.
Orlando Taylor, Dean, Graduate School of Arts and Sciences, Howard University

The African-Americans who responded negatively (to the Oakland proposal) responded out of embarrassment and out of shame. They could not see any value in recognizing that the language of our ancestors was indeed a language. I don't know any other people on the face of the earth who are embarrassed about the language of their ancestors.
Molefi Kete Asante, Chairman, African American Studies Department, Temple University

It seems then that the Oakland school board was merely heeding the words of James Baldwin. In a 1979 *New York Times* essay titled *If Black English Isn't a Language, Then Tell Me, What Is?*, Baldwin observed:

> *It is not the black child's language that is in question, it is not his language that is despised: It is his experience. A child cannot be taught by anyone who despises him, and a child cannot be taught by anyone whose demand, essentially, is that the child repudiate his experience, and all that gives him sustenance, and enter a limbo in which he will no longer be black, and in which he knows that he can never become white. Black people have lost too many black children that way.*[16]

The Western/European worldview is responsible for our believing that language is a tool, and like any tool, requires skill and practice. It is also responsible for us believing that formal rules of grammar (e.g., subject/verb agreement) are necessary to make language coherent. Without the imposition of these arbitrary rules (goose and geese but no moose and meese), communication would supposedly be impossible. Finally, the Western/European worldview is responsible for us believing that language is merely a tool for sharing our thoughts and emotions. Mastery of language is presumably a reflection of our mental faculty. It is the adopting and internalizing of all these beliefs that explains why African-Americans in particular had such a visceral and negative reaction to a resolution that linguists and language scholars unanimously agreed was linguistically sound.

---

[16] Baldwin, J. (1979). If Black English Isn't a Language, Then Tell Me, What Is? *New York Times.* http://www.nytimes.com/books/98/03/29/specials/baldwin-english.html

Five

Language Myths and Colonialism

Myth #1. There are superior and inferior languages (negative and derogatory terms for the latter are creoles, dialects, and pidgins). The reality is that all languages are linguistically promiscuous, meaning all languages are bastards. In fact, without this promiscuity (languages borrowing from other languages), no language would be able to evolve, change, and survive.

The Origins of English

The history of English is conventionally, if perhaps too neatly, divided into three periods usually called Old English (or Anglo-Saxon), Middle English, and Modern English. The earliest period begins with the migration of certain Germanic tribes from the continent to Britain in the fifth century A.D., though no records of their language survive from before the seventh century, and it continues until the end of the eleventh century or a bit later. By that time Latin, Old Norse (the language of the Viking invaders), and especially the Anglo-Norman French of the dominant class after the Norman Conquest in 1066 had begun to have a substantial impact on the lexicon, and the well-developed inflectional system that typifies the grammar of Old English had begun to break down.

The period of Modern English extends from the sixteenth century to our own day. The early part of this period saw the completion of a revolution in the phonology of English that had begun in late Middle English and that effectively redistributed the occurrence of the vowel phonemes to something approximating their present pattern. (Mandeville's English would have sounded even less familiar to us than it looks.)

Other important early developments include the stabilizing effect on spelling of the printing press and the beginning of the direct influence of Latin and, to a lesser extent, Greek on the lexicon. Later, as English came into contact with other cultures around the world and distinctive dialects of English developed in the many areas which Britain had colonized, numerous other languages made small but interesting contributions to our word-stock.

English has what might be called a prehistory as well. As we have seen, our language did not simply spring into existence; it was brought from the Continent by Germanic tribes who had no form of writing and hence left no records. Philologists know that they must have spoken a dialect of a language that can be called West Germanic and that other dialects of this unknown language must have included the ancestors of such languages as German, Dutch, Low German, and Frisian. They know this because of certain systematic similarities which these languages share with each other but do not share with, say, Danish. However, they have had somehow to reconstruct what that language was like in its lexicon, phonology, grammar, and semantics as best they can through sophisticated techniques of comparison developed chiefly during the last century.

Similarly, because ancient and modern languages like Old Norse and Gothic or Icelandic and Norwegian have points in common with Old English and Old High German or Dutch and English that they do not share with French or Russian, it is clear that there was an earlier unrecorded language that can be called simply Germanic and that must be reconstructed in the same way. Still earlier, Germanic was just a dialect (the ancestors of Greek, Latin, and Sanskrit were three other such dialects) of a language conventionally designated Indo-European, and thus English is just one relatively young member of an ancient family of languages whose descendants cover a fair portion of the globe.[17]

Myth #2. Language diversity is a problem. Yet the world most vibrant democracy (India) has over 1,650 languages, including 22 the government has given the status of an official language. In fact, there is no moment in history that makes the case that language diversity is responsible for civilizational discord and disunity. Case in point, neither slavery nor the Holocaust had anything to do with language diversity. Language difference is merely an excuse for human beings to behave badly and cruelly. With enough empathy and compassion all human beings, regardless of our language differences, are capable of coming to understandings that make for peace and cooperation.

Myth #3. Formal language rules are necessary for the development of language. In reality, all of these rules (e.g., subject verb agreement) are arbitrary and unnecessary. All languages biologically share a common set of rules that allow languages to be orderly and linguistically even. Noam Chomsky (1968), Professor of Linguistics and Philosophy, Massachusetts Institute of Technology, and undoubtedly the most distinguished linguist of the twentieth century, contends that all languages follow a fixed set of universal principles of language structure that are biologically determined. As a result, language differences are cultural rather than biological. Chomsky writes, *"My own work leads me to the conclusion that there are far reaching, deep-seated universal principles of language structure. I think we tend to be unaware of them and pay attention only to differentiation of languages because of a very natural response to variety as distinct from the essential shared properties on mankind. . . . I think we will discover that language structures really are uniform. The uniformity results from the existence of fixed, immutable,*

---

[17] Excerpted from Mariam-Webster http://www.merriam-webster.com/help/faq/history.htm

biologically determined principles, which provide the schematism which makes a child capable of organizing and coming to terms with his rather restricted experiences of everyday life and creating complex intellectual structures on that basis" (pp. 127-128).[18]

Chomsky labels this underlying calculus—or set of biologically determined rules and principles—a *Universal Grammar*. But this calculus could also be described as an *attractor*—a self-organizing calculus that exists within all living systems. Attractors give systems symmetry and diversity by noncoercively allowing any naturally occurring system to take on endless possible variations. In this way, rather than limiting, attractors enable.

Myth #4. Language reflects cognitive stature and development. In reality, human development is an emotional, spiritual, relational, communicational, and mental process. We develop our minds by pushing them against the limits of all that we are capable of experiencing and understanding. Nevertheless, Black educators continue to propagate this myth to Black parents. For example, Geoffrey Canada, President and CEO of Harlem Children's Zone, advises that *"even if your child is doing fine in school, you should be looking for extracurricular activities to accelerate your child, because that is what the rest of the parents your child is competing with are doing. . . . We have to think about their (black infants) brains as a computer system that is not wired yet, and it is waiting for us to wire it. And the way we wire that system is by language and stimulation. The more complex the language and stimulation a child is exposed to, the more sophisticated that child's brain wiring will be."* Ronald Ferguson, Director of the Achievement Gap Initiative at Harvard University, also propagates this myth by assuming a link between reading and the development of a child's mind. He claims that research shows that only about 47 percent of college-educated black parents read to their kindergarten-age children daily, compared with 60 percent of similarly educated white parents. Moreover, Ferguson found that college-educated black parents on average had about half as many books in their homes as their white counterparts. Other research reportedly show that by age 4, children of professional parents hear

---

[18] Chomsky, N. (2004). *Language and politics*. Oakland, CA. AK Press.

about 45 million words on average, while children of working-class hear about 26 million, and children of welfare parents hear about 13 million.[19]

Ferguson's point is that reading and vocabulary expansion make for cognitive development. But this is false. Thinking, including how we think and what we think about, is bound up with our worldview. It is our worldview rather than the size of our vocabulary that shapes and influences how we think and what we are capable of thinking about. Indeed, how much of a vocabulary does one need to possess to know that slavery and Jim Crow were moral abominations? Yet how many scholars and university administrators with vast vocabularies supported these institutions? What is especially dangerous about prominent black educators propagating this vocabulary myth is that it reinforces the impression that cognitive stature (as supposedly seen in the size of one's vocabulary) reflects moral capacity. This is simply insulting to all the persons who were brutalized by over 350 years of slavery and Jim Crow. Ultimately, people who have been historically marginalized and brutalized need a new worldview, one that promotes new ways of thinking that make for new worlds. These worlds will be without the cruelty and brutality that has long tortured them and will continue to do so until things have been fundamentally changed.

---

[19] *Essence*, April 2010, pp. 139-146.

Six

Consequences of a Psychology of Colonization

Being colonized constitutes a foreign worldview being either coercively or insidiously imposed on us. Integral to colonization is us coming to the belief that our own worldview is inferior and deficient. It presumably deserves to be displaced, and many local and indigenous persons often try strenuously to do so. But the consequences of doing so are often profound, as to displace a worldview is really to displace a consciousness.

> Self-negation. We become complicit in making many of our own cultural practices that were once moral and natural, immoral and illegal (giving birth using a midwife at home was once a natural process, but now (mostly) illegal; smoking herbs was once a natural process, now illegal; polygamy was once moral and legal, now immoral and illegal; being naked was once natural and moral, now immoral and illegal).

> Self-mutilation. We become complicit in the harming of our own people by supporting laws and regulations that unfairly and disproportionately target our own kind. Drug laws, which

disproportionately target Black people, are a case in point. An overwhelming majority of Black legislators support these laws. Yet these drug laws are decimating the Black community.

✓ One in nine black men was incarcerated on any given day in 2008, with a full 37 percent of young, black, male high school dropouts behind bars (Petitt, 2012).

✓ In just a few decades the U.S. prison population exploded from about 300,000 to over two million. Drug offenses account for two-thirds of the increase in the federal inmate population, and more than half of the increase in the state prison population (Alexander, 2010).

✓ In some states, African Americans comprise 80 to 90 percent of all drug offenders sent to prison. In at least 15 states, blacks are admitted to prison on drug charges at a rate from 20 to 57 times greater than that of white men. Yet African Americans constitute only 15 percent of drug users. A recent study by the National Institute on Drug Abuse reports that white students use cocaine at seven times the rate of black students, use crack cocaine at eight times the rate of black students, and use heroin at seven times the rate of black students (Alexander, 2010).

✓ Nearly 70 percent of young black men will be imprisoned at some point in their lives, and poor black men with low levels of education make up a disproportionate share of incarcerated Americans (Petitt, 2012).

✓ African American youth account for 16 percent of all youth, 28 percent of all juvenile arrests, 35 percent of the youth waived to adult criminal court, and 58 percent of youth admitted to state prison (Alexander, 2010).

✓ In 2005, four out of five drug arrests were for possession, only one out of five for sales. Most people in state prison have no history of violence or even of significant selling activity. During the 1990s — the period of the most aggressive expansion of the drug war — nearly 80 percent of the increase in drug arrests was for marijuana possession, a drug generally considered less harmful than alcohol or tobacco and at least as prevalent in middle-class white communities as in the inner city (Alexander, 2010).

✓ There are more African-Americans under correctional control today — in prison or jail, on probation or parole — than were enslaved in 1850, a decade before the Civil War began (Alexander, 2010).

✓ As of 2004, more African-American men were disenfranchised (due to felon disenfranchisement laws) than in 1870, the year the Fifteenth Amendment was ratified, prohibiting laws that explicitly deny the right to vote on the basis of race (Alexander, 2010).

✓ Taking into account prisoners, a large majority of African-American men in some urban areas have been labeled felons for life, thereby losing the right to vote, legally discriminated against in employment, housing, access to education, and public benefits. In Chicago, the figure is nearly 80 percent (Alexander, 2010).[20]

➢ Self-destruction. The Center for Disease Control and Prevention reports that almost 12 percent of the deaths among Native Americans and Alaska Natives are alcohol-related — more than three times the percentage in the general population. It found 11.7 percent of deaths among Native Americans and Alaska Natives between 2001 and 2005 were alcohol-related, compared with 3.3 percent for the U.S. as a whole. Native American teenagers also have the highest rates of drug-related disorders. Molin Malicay, CEO of the Sonoma County Indian Health Project, believes that cultural factors are one reason drug and alcohol use are disproportionately high amongst Native Americans. *"In general, Native Americans or Indians come from a history of trauma. I had great-grandparents who went through*

---

[20] Excerpted and adapted from Alexander, M. (2010). *The New Jim Crow: Mass incarceration in the age of colorblindness.* New York: New Press; and Petitt, B. (2012). *Invisible men: Mass incarceration and the myth of Black progress.* New York: Russell Sage.

the marches where they were maimed, and there is a lot of hate because of what they have seen. All of that is passed on to us, and it's passed down in many ways. And on the reservations, there's gloom, unemployment, no one works and there is a lot of drinking and a lot of drugs there. You grow up with little hope. It has to do with the environment you live in and history."
Indeed, according to the California Department of Alcohol and Drug Programs, Native American youth who identify with their culture are less likely to abuse drugs.[21]

Conquest & Addiction

Meth abuse rates have reached 30 percent on some rural Indian reservations, and in some Indian communities as many as 65 percent of all documented cases involving child neglect and placement of children in foster care can be traced back to parental involvement with methamphetamine. California Indian Legal Services estimates that in nearly every case they oversee that involves a child being removed from their home, one or both of the parents is using meth. Often in those cases, the baby itself was born with prenatal exposure to the drug.

The Hoopa tribe is no exception.

Hoopa is a 90,000-acre Indian reservation in northern California, nestled in a majestic forested valley carved over thousands of years by the Trinity River. Although the Hoopa people's ancestral territory stretched far beyond the present day reservation boundary, the people feel fortunate to have never been removed from their homeland, a phenomenon experienced by most tribes during the 19th and 20th centuries. The town itself is occupied by about

---

[21] Yeung, B. (2013, November 5). Native American Drug Use Highest Among Teens, New Study Finds. *Huffington Post* (San Francisco). http://www.huffingtonpost. com/2011/11/08/native-american-drug-use-teens_n_1083064.html

3,000 residents, 95 percent of whom self-identify as American Indian according to the 2010 Census.

The broken economy in Hoopa and resulting poverty – the annual household income on the reservation hovers around 13 thousand dollars, and most families receive tribal government assistance – would seem adequate to explain away the high rates of substance abuse. But those in the community with a sense of history say it's much more complicated.

Melodie George-Moore teaches English and Native American literature at Hoopa High School. She's also a leader of traditional Hoopa ceremonies. She believes Hoopa's drug problem has its roots in historical trauma.

"We are a conquered people," George-Moore said. "Unlike any other group in the U.S. we are unique in that respect. That didn't happen to any other group in this country and it continues to happen to this day... In order to understand the pressures people are living under, you have to understand how it looks from a Native perspective to be a conquered people in the U.S."

Multiple generations are grieving the loss of a cherished way of life, a way of life that lasted for thousands of years prior to settlers finding their way to Hoopa. Lessons about events leading to those traumas, said George-Moore, are neither taught in history classes nor spoken about in tribal society at large.

"There's this elephant in the room and we can't talk about it. So it just explodes into all these areas of our lives, because you can't keep all that negativity contained," she said.[22]

---

[22] Excerpted from Hostler, A., & Simas, J. (2012, May). Fixin' up Hoopa: A community's struggle with addiction. *Two Rivers Tribune.* http://www.tworiverstribune. com/2012/05/fixin-up-hoopa-a-communitys-struggle-with-addiction-part-1/

The negative effects of being colonized can be profound. To be colonized is to have our worldviews constantly devalued. However, besides representing how we perceive and make sense of the world, our worldviews also represent how we experience the world. Our worldviews therefore represent every dimension of our being. To have our worldviews constantly devalued is to have our being constantly devalued. This eventually makes for a certain distrust of our being. Trusting our instincts and intuition becomes a problem. An anxiety emerges that is constant and difficult to end. Ultimately, colonialism undermines and compromises our relation to ourselves. We lose the psychological security that is necessary to move comfortably and boldly in a world laden with ambiguity. In compromising and undermining our psychological integrity and security, colonialism makes us vulnerable to all manner of demons and illusions that often make for our undoing.

Seven

Dimensions of Colonialism

B ut why colonization? Why would we want to either violently or insidiously impose our worldview on others? The most popular claim is that colonization is about survival—through colonization we efficiently acquire the human and material resources we supposedly need from other civilizations to improve our own survival and prosperity. Another claim is that colonization neutralizes potential foes, threats, and competitors through assimilation. In sharing the same worldview we presumably come to have the same interests and ambitions.

But there is a psychological dimension to colonization. We colonize so as to save ourselves the hard and difficult work of grappling with the world's boundless human diversity that is found in different cultures and civilizations. Colonization helps lessen this diversity and, consequently, eases the anxiety that comes with human diversity. Thus to colonize is to homogenize, to make others believe and experience the world like we do for our own selfish purposes. However, colonization is contrary to the world's natural order and rhythms.

> ➤ Colonization removes and lessens human diversity. Human diversity reflects the world's natural order. The world is always striving to produce and promote diversity. Life flourishes through the promotion of diversity. Thus by aiming to reduce

human diversity, colonization constitutes a threat to life. It violates the world's natural order.

> Colonization dehumanizes us. Colonization assumes that the condition of our own humanity is separate from the condition of others' humanity. But this is false. There is no separation between human beings. We are relational rather than individual beings. We shape our humanity out of the relational resources that others make available to us. Thus colonization dehumanizes both sides, those doing the colonizing and those being colonized. As Frederick Douglass once said, "No man can put a chain about the ankle of his fellow man without at last finding the other end fastened about his own neck."

Eight

Resisting Colonialism

There is much history that shows different peoples being colonized and acting accordingly. But there is also much history revealing people contesting and resisting colonialism.

Decolonizing The Mind

In 2005, eight Indigenous intellectuals created the volume For Indigenous Eyes Only: A Decolonization Handbook, to offer hands-on suggestions and activities for Indigenous communities to engage in as they worked to develop decolonizing activities. Beginning from the assumption that Indigenous Peoples have the power, strength, and intelligence to develop culturally specific decolonization strategies to pursue our own strategies of liberation, we attempted to begin to demystify the language of colonization and decolonization. Through a step-by-step process, we hoped to help Indigenous readers identify useful concepts, terms, and intellectual frameworks that will assist all of us in our struggle toward meaningful change and self-determination. The handbook covered a wide range of topics including Indigenous governance, education, languages, oral tradition, repatriation, images and stereotypes, nutritional strategies, and truthtelling.

"The most potent weapon in the hands of the oppressor is the mind of the oppressed."
—Steve Biko

In this volume, a number of new Indigenous scholars, writers, and activists have collaborated for the creation of a sequel to the Decolonization Handbook. The title, For Indigenous Minds Only, reflects an understanding that decolonizing actions must begin in the mind, and that creative, consistent, decolonized thinking shapes and empowers the brain, which in turn provides a major prime for positive change. Undoing the effects of colonialism and working toward decolonization requires each of us to consciously consider to what degree we have been affected by not only the physical aspects of colonization, but also the psychological, mental, and spiritual aspects. Kenyan intellectual Ngugi wa Thiong'o, in his book Decolonising the Mind, describes the "cultural bomb" as the greatest weapon unleashed by imperialism:

The effect of the cultural bomb is to annihilate a people's belief in their names, in their languages, in their environment, in their heritage of struggle, in their unity, in their capacities and ultimately in themselves. It makes them see their past as one wasteland of non-achievement and it makes them want to distance themselves from that wasteland. It makes them want to identify with that which is furthest removed from themselves; for instance, with other peoples' languages rather than their own. It makes them identify with that which is decadent and reactionary, all those forces that would stop their own springs of life. It even plants serious doubts about the moral righteousness of struggle. Possibilities of triumph or victory are seen as remote, ridiculous dreams. The intended results are despair, despondency and a collective death-wish.

The planting and igniting of this "cultural bomb" by the colonizing forces has been essential to the colonization process, for if our minds *are contaminated with self-hatred and the belief that we are inferior to our colonizers, we will believe in both the necessity and virtue of our own colonization. We will begin to diminish the wisdom and beauty of Indigenous ways of being and embrace the ways of the colonizers as inherently superior. When we believe in their superiority, our motivation to fight for our own liberation is splintered and eventually seriously damaged. However, we do not believe that it can be killed. That destiny lies within each of us. Still, if we accept the cultural bomb, why would we fight for something we perceive to be undesirable?*

Working toward decolonization, then, requires us to consciously and critically assess how our minds have been affected by the cultural bomb of colonization. Only then will we be positioned to take action that reflects a rejection of the programming of self-hatred with which we have been indoctrinated. We will also learn to assess the claims of colonizer society regarding its justification for colonization and its sense of superiority. When we regain a belief in the wisdom and beauty of our traditional ways of being and reject the colonial lies that have inundated us, we will release the pent-up dreams of liberation and again realize the need for resistance to colonization. This volume is dedicated to facilitating the critical thinking that will help us work toward our collective decolonization.

Definitions of Colonization and Decolonization

Colonization generally refers to the process that is perpetuated after the initial control over Indigenous Peoples is achieved through invasion and conquest. Perpetuating colonization allows the colonizers to maintain or expand their social, political, and economic power. It is detrimental to us because their power comes at the expense of Indigenous lands, resources, lives, and self-determination. Not only has colonization resulted in the loss of major rights such as land and self-determination, most of our contemporary daily struggles are also a direct consequence of colonization (poverty, family violence, chemical dependency, suicide, health deterioration). Colonization is an all-encompassing presence in our lives.

Decolonization is the meaningful and active resistance to the forces of colonialism that perpetuate the subjugation and/or exploitation of our minds, bodies, and lands. Its ultimate purpose is to overturn the colonial structure and realize Indigenous liberation. First and foremost, decolonization must occur in our own minds. The Tunisian decolonization activist, Albert Memmi, wrote, "In order for the colonizer to be the complete master, it is not enough for him to be so in actual fact, he must also believe in its legitimacy. In order for that legitimacy to be complete, it is not enough for the colonized to be a slave, he must also accept his role." The first step toward decolonization, then, is to question the legitimacy of colonization. Once we recognize the truth of this injustice, we can think about ways to resist and challenge colonial institutions and ideologies. Thus, decolonization is not passive, but rather it requires something called praxis.

In accepting the premise of colonization and working toward decolonization, we are not relegating ourselves to a status as victim, but rather we are actively working toward our own freedom to transform our lives and the world around us. The project that begins with our minds, therefore, has revolutionary potential.

Michael Yellow Bird has created a Conceptual Model of Decolonization in which he defines decolonization as both an event and a process:

Event – As an event, decolonization concerns reaching a level of critical consciousness, an active understanding that you are (or have been) colonized and are thus responding to life circumstances in ways that are limited, destructive, and externally controlled.

Process – As a process, decolonization means engaging in the activities of creating, restoring, and birthing. It means creating and consciously using various strategies to liberate oneself, adapt to or survive oppressive conditions; it means restoring cultural practices, thinking, beliefs, and values that were taken away or abandoned but are still relevant and necessary to survival; and it means the birthing of new ideas, thinking, technologies, and lifestyles that contribute to the advancement and empowerment of Indigenous Peoples.

As Indigenous Peoples we know that this devastation has been occurring on Turtle Island for the last five centuries; and, for that length of time, our ancestors have continued to sound the alarm to the ongoing, un-restrained feeding frenzy of non-renewable resources by the corporate-led, capitalist engines of colonial society. We know from the stories and prophecies of our ancestors that this mindless consumption activity portends a future of deep hardship and dramatic change for all forms of life on the earth. We are now bearing witness to the collapse of major ecosystems, the extinction of many species, the desertification of fertile lands, the rise in infectious diseases, a decline in fisheries, and a staggering increase in the toxicity of the lands, waters, and air.

Moreover, we now have become even more aware of how this collapse is contributing to the suffering of all Indigenous life. What is happening now differs from the natural declines of species and changes to the earth in that the planet has now reached a "tipping point" that will undoubtedly threaten the foundations of industrial civilization and the survival of much of life. The whole earth will reap the effects of hyper-exploitation, exceeding the carrying capacity, and wide-scale ecological degradation or destruction. To be clear, this present and impending disaster was not the making of our ancestors who maintained ingenious, sustainable ways of life—ways that were considered to be backward, primitive, and undeveloped by our colonizers. Still, the cultural bomb has infected many, but not all, Indigenous Peoples in the current generation, making us apologists and cheerleaders for the unfettered corporatocracy that continues to bring about the rapid decline of our planet. Our uncritical participation in this colonial system undoubtedly increases the rate at which we are falling and failing.

Thus, when we discuss strategies for decolonization, we also cannot afford to ignore our current predicament. While addressing colonialism in our lives, it is important for us to understand how that struggle influences, interacts with, and is affected by these other global emergencies. It is an awareness of these impending crises that must foreground all our visions, thoughts, and actions related to decolonization. All of this means that as Indigenous people, we can no longer pretend that it is in our best interest to get on board with the project of modernity and economic development as a pathway to self-determination. That ship is quickly sinking.

We recognize that our efforts build on the efforts of generations of Indigenous people who came before us—people who resisted colonization on their watch, in their own way. We are attempting to carry on that five-hundred-year-old tradition in defense of our homelands and Peoples. We do not claim to provide universal solutions, nor do we think that every community suffers from identical problems. What we do know is that colonized populations tend to suffer similar effects of colonization and share common struggles.

For more than five hundred years, Indigenous populations have experienced the ravages of imperial powers as they annihilated our people and plundered our homelands. We observed the insanity, knowing it was suicidal to destroy the earth in that manner, and we knew that kind of pillaging could not continue indefinitely. Now, the failure of colonizer ways is written in every collapsing economy, every effect of climate change, and in every "peak" fossil fuel. Never before has the untenable nature of colonialism been so apparent here on Turtle Island. Colonial rule will come to an end. We need to prepare to take back our freedom.[23]

---

[23] Excerpted from Waziyatawin and Michael Yellow Bird's Introduction, *For Indigenous Minds Only: A Decolonization Handbook.*

Nine

On the Origins of a European/Western Epistemology

Knowing a worldview begins with knowing the names and figures responsible for forging and sculpting the epistemology that is of that worldview. In the case of the Western/European epistemology that rules academe, such figures are distinctly of a certain gender and race—e.g., Descartes, Locke, Hume, Nietzsche, Foucault, Habermas, Derrida, Bacon, Newton, Galileo, Socrates, Plato, Aristotle, Kant, Mill, Bentham, Goffman, Freud, Einstein, and Wittgenstein.

These figures produced the seminal texts—the supposed classics—that must be read and engaged with in order to acquire the expertise, knowledge, and credentials necessary to produce and disseminate what our worldview defines as knowledge. These are the figures and texts that shape our curriculums and are usually listed as required readings in syllabi. Thus these figures and texts play an integral role in shaping how we create, legitimize, and organize what we define as knowledge. Any attempt to disrupt the influence of these figures and texts normally makes for controversy, as opponents are seen as undermining the very foundation of Western/European civilization and propagating the belief that Other civilizations have comparable figures and texts deserving of equal attention.

Core Knowledge

Columbia University has taken the next step in its plan to add new multicultural classes to its core curriculum, the great books undergraduate program.

Columbia is assigning a young professor of Western civilization, Roosevelt Montas, 34, to direct the effort.

The position will involve balancing the concerns of academics who worry that the university could veer from its focus on a canon of Western texts and students who have been pushing the university to make the core curriculum, called the Core, more inclusive.

Mr. Montas, a Dominican immigrant who moved to New York in his teens and attended Columbia as a scholarship student, is quick to acknowledge that his ethnic and economic background "embodies diversity," which some believe is missing from the core curriculum. Yet he is also one of the Core's most passionate defenders.

"I don't represent the tradition of dead white males that the Core is associated with," Mr. Montas said of his new role. "I think it helps to undo or challenge the idea that this is a white curriculum.

"But the idea that a core curriculum ought to be representative based on the way that, say, Congress is representative, that it should be demographically representative, that's just apples and oranges," he said. "The core curriculum represents and embodies the most important ideas that have shaped the institutions and values of our culture. And it ought to represent those ideas."

Mr. Montas, who teaches a Core class on contemporary civilization that surveys Western moral and political thought, beginning with Plato, said being somewhere in the middle of the often heated debate on the curriculum makes him well-positioned to mend the rift between the two sides.

He used the same word to describe his first two years at Columbia. "I doubt there are very many people who enter college in the same state of bewilderment and ignorance that I did. The core curriculum worked very well for me because I was trying to make sense of the world into which I was thrust," he said. That world, he acknowledged, was mostly white and upper class.

He wrote a master's degree thesis on Plato and his doctoral dissertation on abolitionism and national identity, and has presented papers on such topics as the challenge of "Moby Dick" to race and gender.

But he was quick to add of the Core: "It's a systematic and rigorous approach to some of the fundamental questions about what it means to be human — questions that every human being must ask his or herself. They have been asked over and over again in history."

That philosophy of the core curriculum will likely sit well with conservative academics like the administrators of the Intercollegiate Studies Institute, who have lauded Columbia's great books program and have criticized other universities, such as Harvard, that have moved away from the approach.

"We wouldn't want any effort to water that down, or to succumb to some political pressure," the institute's director of university stewardship, Richard Brake, said. "We don't want some kind of very rigid multicultural perspective." As long as the plan is not to replace Shakespeare with Eastern philosophy texts, however, Mr. Brake said the institute has no complaints with strengthening supplementary multicultural offerings.

Mr. Montas said the structure of the core curriculum will not change. Undergraduate students will still have to take a set of 12 classes, *including two Western civilization courses, literature, art, and music humanities, a writing class, two science classes, a foreign language, and a choice of one class in a "major" non-Western culture.*

Mr. Montas added that he is confident that the debate over what belongs in the Core and what does not will not end there. "The core curriculum is always evolving and it has to evolve," he said. "Perhaps a better way of putting it is that the core curriculum is not a tradition of thought but a tradition of debate."[24]

In most introductory courses, such as foundational communication and rhetoric courses, various foundational texts are required reading so as to introduce students to the seminal figures that define the discipline.

A Syllabus
Introduction To Rhetoric

Texts

- *Kitto: The Greeks. This text gives us an introduction to the ancient Greek world, its history, geography, people, and cultural assumptions.*
- *Connor: Greek Orations 4th Century B.C. This collection includes ancient Greek speeches by Lysias, Isocrates, Demosthenes, Aeschines, Hyperides, and the Letter of Philip II of Macedon.*
- *Plato: Gorgias. This is Plato's attack on the way rhetoric was practiced in his day. One of the characters in the dialogue is Gorgias, a famous teacher of the art of rhetoric.*
- *Plato: Phaedrus. The counterpart to the Gorgias, this dialogue offers Plato's conception of a noble rhetoric. We will read this along with Weaver's assessment of the dialogue and its relation to rhetoric.*

---

[24] Excerpted from Garland, S. (2008, April 14). Columbia professor takes on overhaul of core curriculum. *The Sun*. http://www.nysun.com/new-york/columbia-professor-takes-on-overhaul-of-core/

- *Aristotle: On Rhetoric.* This is George Kennedy's translation of Aristotle's work. As a text, On Rhetoric sets the standard for classical assumptions about rhetoric.
- *Cicero: Murder Trials.* As the major Roman rhetorical theorist, most of Cicero's theory is a reworking and extension of Aristotle; we'll talk about these works. Unlike Aristotle, however, Cicero was a master orator who was especially keen at defense pleadings. Michael Grant has translated several of Cicero's forensic speeches.
- *Quintilian: On the Teaching of Speaking and Writing.* This is a translation by James J. Murphy of Books I, II, and X of Institutio Oratoria, Quintilian's major treatise on rhetorical education.
- *On Reserve in the library: Matsen, Rollinson, Sousa: Readings from Classical Rhetoric.* This contains the readings for the progymnasmata (3), one reading from the ad Herennium, and several short selections from Cicero. Bizzell & Herzberg: The Rhetorical Tradition. This contains readings for Isocrates--Against the Sophists, Antidosis--and the primary material in the ad Herennium.

Course Description and Requirements

In studying rhetorical theory from classical times, we are looking at the history of this and related disciplines. We will be asking about the meaning of the term rhetoric, the way scholars and practitioners throughout the ages have viewed rhetoric as a way of knowing and as a way of being. We focus on classical rhetoric as the foundation of the theories that saw major modification in the 18th century and again during contemporary times. Our focus is on the ancient Greek and Roman discussions of the art of rhetoric. If you have taken a public speaking class, you have been exposed to Aristotle's On Rhetoric. Most public speaking texts are merely modernized versions of the classical theories of argument, organization, style and delivery--rhetoric--which Aristotle cataloged in his famous book. You probably learned about the three kinds of *proof or what constitutes lively and appropriate style. These are principles of rhetoric whose foundations, in the Western world, are in ancient Greek and Roman writings and practices.*

It is important to have these basic ideas firmly in our minds because so much of how we now explore issues of rhetoric and communication is a result of past theories. In some ways, this class, to our discipline, is like a beginning language class. Before you can speak Chinese or French, you must learn the structure of the language and begin to build basic vocabulary. You'll never speak a foreign language if you only have a vague sense of the terms; saying a word that kind of sounds like the one you want will not work. Similarly, having a vague sense of how Plato, Aristotle, Cicero, or Quintilian define the essence of persuasion will not work. This is about the only class in the department where I think flash cards might be useful. We memorize, not for the exercise, but because we need to get beyond a general understanding to appreciate and critique our contemporary response to rhetorical/communication issues. There is no escaping the need to know the details; just as any third year language student should get 100% on a first year vocabulary test, you need to have the classical theories down cold before we turn to modifications of these classical works in our courses in the department.

Our texts, with the exception of Kitto's book, are primary works. Sometimes the language/style of another time makes reading more difficult. You will need to adjust to a different sentence structure. It may help to read a passage aloud. Work at your reading; do not give up. All of you are capable of reading, with understanding, all of these works. This is not, however, the kind of material which can be read once only, amidst distractions, or quickly. Do not postpone. If a reading is assigned for Monday it needs to be read for Monday. You need to come to class ready to explain what you read, not waiting for someone else to lead you through the material. If you fall behind it will be difficult to catch up. The load gets lighter only once you break through initial resistance to this kind of dense writing. Theory is enjoyable once you master it. There is no piece in the text whose style is as convoluted as some contemporary theorists (Heidegger, for example).

The class will be structured in such a way that careful preparation on your part is necessary. We will have pop quizzes (yes, they'll count), memory bees, etc. Previous classes have told me that more quizzes were needed; I shall keep that in mind. I'll give you the cultural context and historical perspective for the theories. I'll answer questions and draw connections between theorists, but you must teach yourself through reading and questioning. It will be a challenging semester. You'll have "fun" only if you work at it and work with me.

The texts for the course have limited background information. We will have discussion leaders and reading guides for the theorists we will be studying this semester. For the theory for which you will be the expert you will be expected to prepare a reading guide for the class, initiate the class discussion, prepare several discussion questions or construct exercises that help us go through the material, and make sure we "learn" the important concepts. The assignment will be graded. Both sections of the course have the same assignments and basic schedule. You may find it helpful to form study groups which include students from both classes who are working on a particular reading.

The library has a good collection of books on rhetorical theory in general and on the particular theorists we will be working with this semester. Some books will deal with the author of a particular reading, some will be critiques of that person's theory, yet others will place the times in context. Probably the best information will come from articles in our disciplinary periodicals. You should acquaint yourself with Philosophy and Rhetoric, Quarterly Journal of Speech, and the regional journals, esp.,

Southern Journal of Speech Communication, Western Journal of Speech Communication, and Communication Studies which was formerly Central States Speech Journal. You will find it helpful to read this material as we go along, even if the period is not one where you are the expert, because it will help you understand the meaning of the term rhetoric. Ask yourself what epistemological and ontological questions were addressed as you complete your reading of each theorist.

We are left with the impression from most introductory communication and rhetoric syllabuses that no African, Asian, Middle Eastern, or Native American civilization had any knowledge of rhetoric and communication that is even comparable to that of the Greeks and thereby deserving to be on any list of required readings. Apparently, only the Greeks were thinking deeply about the affairs of the world and trying to develop a knowledge that was universally reliable and valuable. For where are the seminal African, Native American, Asian, and Middle Eastern thinkers in our introductory communication texts and syllabuses? However, as much as the impression of African, Asian, Native American, and Middle Eastern civilizations being devoid of any valuable knowledge of communication is false, often impression—rather than reality—is what matters in the end.

Do Europeans Own Philosophy?

Why is it that if Mozart sneezes it is "music" but the most sophisticated Indian music ragas are the subject of "ethnomusicology"?

Is that "ethnos" not also applicable to the philosophical thinking that Indian philosophers practice - so much so that their thinking is more the subject of Western European and North American anthropological fieldwork and investigation?

We can turn around and look at Africa. What about thinkers like Henry Odera Oruka, Ngugi wa Thiong'o, Wole Soyinka,

Chinua Achebe, Okot p'Bitek, Taban Lo Liyong, Achille Mbembe, Emmanuel Chukwudi Eze, Souleymane Bachir Diagne, V.Y. Mudimbe: Would they qualify for the term "philosopher" or "public intellectuals" perhaps, or is that also "ethnophilosophy"?

Why is European philosophy "philosophy", but African philosophy ethnophilosophy, the way Indian music is ethnomusic - an ethnographic logic that is based on the very same reasoning that if you were to go to the New York Museum of Natural History (popularised in Shawn Levy's Night at the Museum [2006]), you only see animals and non-white peoples and their cultures featured inside glass cages, but no cage is in sight for white people and their cultures - they just get to stroll through the isles and enjoy the power and ability of looking at taxidermic Yaks, cave dwellers, elephants, Eskimos, buffalo, Native Americans, etc, all in a single winding row.

The same ethnographic gaze is evident in the encounter with the intellectual disposition of the Arab or Muslim world: Azmi Bishara, Sadeq Jalal Al-Azm, Fawwaz Traboulsi, Abdallah Laroui, Michel Kilo, Abdolkarim Soroush. The list of prominent thinkers is endless.

In Japan, Kojan Karatani, in Cuba, Roberto Fernandez Retamar, or even in the United States people like Cornel West, whose thinking is not entirely in the European continental tradition - what about them? Where do they fit in? Can they think - is what they do also thinking, philosophical, pertinent, perhaps, or is that also suitable for ethnographic examinations?

The question of Eurocentricism is now entirely blasé. Of course Europeans are Eurocentric and see the world from their vantage point, and why should they not? They are the inheritors of multiple (now defunct) empires and they still carry within them the phantom hubris of those empires and they think their particular philosophy is "philosophy" and their particular thinking is "think-ing", and everything else is - as the great European philosopher Immanuel Levinas was wont of saying - "dancing".

The question is rather the manner in which non-European think-ing can reach self-consciousness and evident universality, not at the cost of whatever European philosophers may think of them-selves for the world at large, but for the purpose of offering alter-native (complementary or contradictory) visions of reality more rooted in the lived experiences of people in Africa, in Asia, in Latin America - counties and climes once under the spell of the thing that calls itself "the West" but happily no more.

The trajectory of contemporary thinking around the globe is not spontaneously conditioned in our own immediate time and disparate locations, but has a much deeper and wider spectrum that goes back to earlier generations of thinkers ranging from José Marti to Jamal al-Din al-Afghani, to Aime Cesaire, W.E.B. DuBois, Liang Qichao, Frantz Fanon, Rabindranath Tagore, Mahatma Gandhi, etc.

There is thus a direct and unmitigated structural link between an empire, or an imperial frame of reference, and the presumed uni-versality of a thinker thinking in the bosoms of that empire.

As all other people, Europeans are perfectly entitled to their own self-centrism.

But that globality is no more - people from every clime and conti-nent are up and about claiming their own cosmopolitan worldli-ness and with it their innate ability to think beyond the confine-ments of that Eurocentricism, which to be sure is still entitled to its phantom pleasures of thinking itself the centre of the uni-verse. The Gramscian superimposed "similar conditions" are now emerging in multiple cites of the liberated humanity.

The world at large, and the Arab and Muslim world in particular, is going through world historic changes - these changes have produced thinkers, poets, artists, and public intellectuals at the centre of their moral and political imagination - all thinking and acting in terms at once domestic to their immediate geography and yet global in its consequences.

Compared to those liberating tsunamis now turning the world upside down, cliché-ridden assumption about Europe and its increasingly provincialised philosophical pedigree is a tempest in the cup. Reduced to its own fair share of the humanity at large, and like all other continents and climes, Europe has much to teach the world, but now on a far more leveled and democratic playing field, where its philosophy is European philosophy not "Philosophy", [and]its music European music not "Music".[25]

---

[25] Excerpted from Dabashi, H. (2013, January 15). Can non-Europeans think? *Al Jazeera.* http://www.aljazeera.com/indepth/opinion/2013/01/2013114142638797542.html

Ten

Colonialism, Metaphors, and Communication

No worldview is devoid of conflict, tension, and diversity, which means that no worldview can be defined completely and definitively, or reduced to a kind of singularity. To label a worldview is to refer to a broad description of features and processes that seem common to that worldview within a certain time and space. Worldviews are always changing because human beings are always changing as result of having to deal with a world that is laden with ambiguity. The Western/ European worldview begins on the belief (ontology) that the world is of a conflict between opposing (positive and negative) forces.

- ✓ Good vs. Evil
- ✓ Mind vs Body
- ✓ Life vs. Death
- ✓ Local vs. Alien
- ✓ Order vs. Chaos
- ✓ Health vs. Illness
- ✓ Light vs. Darkness
- ✓ Peace vs. Violence
- ✓ Meaning vs. Ambiguity
- ✓ Knowledge vs. Ignorance

✓ Homogeneity vs. Diversity
✓ Communication vs. Confusion

Worldviews also give us our metaphors which in turn solidify our worldviews. We conceive, perceive, experience, organize, and relate to the world through metaphors. It is because of metaphors that language matters. The notion that language shapes our social worlds should really be metaphors shape our social worlds. In influencing how we conceive things, metaphors influence how we perceive and make sense of things. For example, in a review of media representations, David Cisneros (2008) found that *"Metaphors of immigrants often portray them as objects or threats to society, whether biological, physical, or social. On the other hand, metaphors of immigration concretize the problem through cognitive comparisons to other physical or social ills"* (p. 573).[26] Who controls what metaphors we use to describe and perceive things wields much influence in shaping what we experience as real. In the European/Western worldview, the dominant metaphors deal with War (war on drugs, war on poverty, war on crime, war on terror, war on the middle class, war on cancer, war on illegal immigration) and Machines (viewing our minds as computers, or viewing an organization or a team as a well-oiled machine).

The War On Cancer

Duke University doctors have successfully dropped the first "smart bomb" on breast cancer, using a drug to deliver a toxic payload to tumor cells while leaving healthy ones alone.

In a key test involving nearly 1,000 women with very advanced disease, the experimental treatment extended by several months the time women lived without their cancer getting worse, doctors planned to report Sunday at a cancer conference in Chicago.

---

[26] Cisneros, D. (2008). Contaminated communities: The metaphor of "immigrant as pollutant" in media representations of immigration. *Rhetoric & Public Affairs*, *11*, 569-602.

More importantly, the treatment seems likely to improve survival; it will take more time to know for sure. After two years, 65 percent of women who received it were still alive versus 47 percent of those in a comparison group given two standard cancer drugs.

That margin fell just short of the very strict criteria researchers set for stopping the study and declaring the new treatment a winner, and they hope the benefit becomes more clear with time. In fact, so many women on the new treatment are still alive that researchers cannot yet determine average survival for the group.

"The absolute difference is greater than one year in how long these people live," said the study's leader, Dr. Kimberly Blackwell of Duke University. "This is a major step forward."

Researchers combined Herceptin with a chemotherapy so toxic that it can't be given by itself, plus a chemical to keep the two linked until they reach a cancer cell where the poison can be released to kill it.

This double weapon, called T-DM1, is the "smart bomb," although it's actually not all that smart – Herceptin isn't a homing device, just a substance that binds to breast cancer cells once it encounters them.

"The data are pretty compelling," said Dr. Michael Link, a pediatric cancer specialist at Stanford University who is president of the American Society of Clinical Oncology, the group hosting the Chicago conference where the results were being presented.

"It's sort of a smart bomb kind of therapy, a poison delivered to the tumor ... and not a lot of other collateral damage to other organs," he said.[27]

Metaphors of War and Machine in Communication Studies

Metaphors of war and machine fundamentally shape our common understanding of communication in the western world. Arguments must be "won" and opposing arguments "shut down," "crushed," "demolished," and "annihilated." Certain arguments

---

[27] Excerpted from Marchione, M. (2012, June 3). Study: 'Smart bomb' drug attacks breast cancer. *Associated Press*.

are "indefensible" and every weak point must be "attacked" and shown to be "riddled" with holes. We contend that communication has "broken down" and "lines" of communication need to open up. Good communication is presumably about persons "clicking" and being on the same "wavelength." Like a machine, communication presumably has different components (sender, receiver, medium, message) that demand organization, coordination, and standardization in order to work properly and effectively. Machines must function smoothly. There can be no disruption, conflict, and diversity. Homogeneity is vital, as in the need for persons to share a common language and preferably share a common set of experiences so both sender and receiver can presumably know what each other means. Indeed, the machine metaphor in communication can be seen in every legislative initiative to make English the official language of the United States, and our demand that every person *Speak English*. The underlying fear is that language diversity will bring confusion, conflict, and disunity. It will presumably disrupt the country from working smoothly.

This fear of language diversity is explicit in the writings of Samuel Huntington, once Chairman of the Harvard Academy for International and Area Studies, and Albert J. Weatherhead III University Professor at Harvard University. In *Who We Are: The Challenges to America's National Identity*, Huntington (2004) calls for a new push to protect the "American Creed."[28] According to Huntington, the "American Creed," as initially formulated by Thomas Jefferson and elaborated upon by many others, "is widely viewed" as the defining element of American identity. This Creed, argues Huntington, "was the product of the distinct Anglo-Protestant culture of the founding settlers of America in the seventeenth and eighteenth centuries." Huntington claims that key elements of that culture include, "the English language; Christianity; religious commitment; English concepts of the rule of law, responsibility of rulers, and the rights of individuals; and the dissenting Protestant values of individualism, the work ethic,

---

[28] Huntington, S. (2004). *Who We Are: The Challenges to America's National Identity*. New York: Simon & Schuster.

and the belief that humans have the ability and duty to try to create a heaven on earth" (pp. xv-xvi). Huntington believes that in the face of September 11, "Americans should recommit themselves to the Anglo-Protestant culture, traditions, and values that for three and half centuries have been embraced by Americans of all races, ethnicities, and religions and that have been the source of their liberty, unity, power, prosperity, and moral leadership as a force for good in the world" (p. xvii).

Huntington claims that Latino immigration poses the greatest threat to the territorial, cultural, and political integrity of the United States. According to Huntington, "the American people who achieved independence in the late eighteenth century were few and homogenous: overwhelmingly white (thanks to the exclusion of blacks and Indians from citizenship), British and Protestant, broadly sharing a common culture, and overwhelmingly committed to the political principles embodied in the Declaration of Independence, the Constitution, and other founding documents" (p. 11). Huntington calls for immediate and severe actions to neutralize all of these threats. He believes that these threats constitute the greatest challenge to our "existing cultural, political, legal, commercial, and educational systems," and "to the historical, cultural, and linguistic identity" of the U.S.

The machine metaphor pervades *intercultural* communication—a major field of study within communication studies. Human diversity is assumed to be a problem that needs to be managed properly out of fear of it causing conflict and disruption. McDaniel, Samovar, and Porter (2006), authors of one of the most intercultural communication textbooks, claim that "The international community is riven with sectarian violence arising from ideological, cultural, and racial differences" (p. 15). Neuliep (2000), also an author of a highly popular intercultural communication textbook, writes, "history tells an ugly story of what happens when people of diverse cultural, ethnic, religious, or linguistic backgrounds converge in one place" (p. 2). Consequently, in regards to language diversity, Samovar, Porter, and McDaniel (2007) claim that "language diversity presents a problem in the United States" and "that knowledge of English and the ability to communicate in English are essential in American society" (pp. 182-183). The suspicion of language diversity emerges from the fact the intercultural communication generally defines communication as a linguistic and symbolic process, which means that sharing a common set of codes and symbols (language) is assumed to be necessary for communication.

Neuliep (2000) claims that "Intercultural communication occurs whenever a minimum of two persons from different cultures or microcultures come together and exchange verbal and nonverbal symbols" (p. 18). Similarly, Klopf and McCroskey (2007) hold that "communication is the process by which persons share information, meanings, and feelings through the exchange of verbal and nonverbal messages" (p. 34). For Samovar, Porter, and McDaniel (2007), "communication is the process through which symbols are transmitted for the purpose of eliciting a response" (p. 12). Indeed, most intercultural communication textbooks forward definitions of communication that assume no profound relationship between communication and the human condition, or even between communication and the condition of the world. Consistent with popular definitions of communication, communication is cast as a tool to share our thoughts and emotions, and communication competency is about mastery of various skills and techniques.

Intercultural communication texts, courses, and discourses generally assume a common set of definitions of intercultural communication. *"Intercultural communication generally involves face-to-face communication between people from different national cultures." "Intercultural communication occurs when large and important cultural differences create dissimilar interpretations and expectations about how to communicate competently."* Intercultural communication is supposedly communication between peoples of different cultures. Intercultural communication texts and courses generally focus on introducing us to the features and attributes of different cultures. As Klopf and McCroskey (2007) note, "Unless we know the rules of other cultures' practices, we will discover it is almost impossible to tell how members of other cultures will behave in similar situations" (p. 22).[29] We learn in popular intercultural communication texts that whereas some cultures are high context (emphasis on nonverbal communication), others are low context (focus on verbal communication), and whereas some cultures are feminine, others are masculine, and whereas some cultures are collectivist, others are individualist, and whereas some cultures are patriarchal, others are matriarchal, and whereas some cultures are monochromic, others are polychromic, and whereas some cultures are active, others are passive, and whereas some cultures as vertical, others are horizontal, and whereas some cultures are universalist, others are particularist, and whereas some cultures are instrumental, others are expressive, and whereas some cultures are associative, others are abstractive, and so forth. We are encouraged to use this knowledge of how cultures are different to navigate and manage our relations with persons of different cultures. Intercultural communication assumes that our failure to successfully manage and navigate our differences—by lacking knowledge of each other's differences—is what makes for conflict, tension, and disruption. Thus knowledge of different cultures is supposedly vital for the cultivation of *good* intercultural communication.

Popular definitions of intercultural communication also assume that communication is a medium through which persons of different cultures interact with each other. Both sides should presumably know how the other side uses words, symbols, and language. We should know what different behaviors and actions mean for different peoples. We should also presumably know the meanings behind various customs and traditions. Such knowledge is presumably vital to *good* intercultural communication. Intercultural communication texts and courses devote considerable attention to how different cultures use words, symbols, and language. The goal is to save us from ignorantly saying or doing

---

[29] Klopf, D. W., & McCroskey, J. C. (2007). *Intercultural communication encounters.* Boston, MA: Pearson.

McDaniel, E. R., Samovar, L. A., & Porter, R. E. (2006). *Intercultural communication.* Belmont, CA: Thomson Wadsworth.

Neuliep, J. W. (2000). *Intercultural communication: A contextual approach.* Boston, MA: Houghton Mifflin.

Samovar, L. A., Porter, R. E., & McDaniel, E. R. (2007). *Communication between cultures.* Belmont, CA: Thomson Wadsworth

something *offensive* that will make for conflict and discord. Ultimately, like a machine, intercultural communication strives to avoid friction and disruption by removing all of the differences that supposedly cause friction and disruption.

Every intercultural communication text promises to give us the knowledge that will allow us to effectively manage and navigate each other's differences. This is the mission of intercultural communication—to use communication to lessen the threat of our differences. We read in popular intercultural communication texts that *"The world is experiencing new forms of conflict . . . . Some of these are overt military actions and some of them are covert statements of protest. Many of these conflicts arise from cross-cultural tensions, cross-border political goals and tensions arising from multi-ethnic, multi-religious populations. To date, neither mainstream media nor scholarly debate has successfully addressed the issue of how modern conflicts affect intercultural communication both at the theoretical level as well as at the level of specific case studies. In order to curb the flaring up of conflicts or for conflicts to come to sustainable, creative endings, it is important to bring to public attention the key uses and contributions of intercultural communication."*

We also have intercultural communication workshops with titles like *"Communicating in a Cross-Cultural Environment—Skills for Working and Living in a Multicultural World"* that come with the following descriptions: *"How do cultural differences create barriers for effective communication? What cultural values do we have that affect how we interact with others, especially those from differing cultural backgrounds? What skills are useful when working with people from different cultural backgrounds? What is the role of these cultural differences in addressing interpersonal conflicts? Our interactions with the world are shaped by our cultural values and understandings. This workshop will seek to address the above questions through a broad analysis of cultural values and understandings, and a focus on identifying barriers that prevent effective cross-cultural communication. Emphasis will be placed on developing and practicing skills that will aid in decreasing the effects of these barriers."* In both intercultural communication textbooks and courses, the belief is reinforced that without finding effective ways to deal with our differences, strife and conflict will arise and throw the world into chaos and mayhem. For intercultural communication the goal is convergence, as in both sides agreeing to abide by a common set of rules and expectations. It is presumably this commonality—rather than our diversity—that will allow us to live and work in harmony with each. In this way, the mission of intercultural communication is *really* to find the most effective means to neutralize our differences so as to keep the system (the machine) running smoothly. This mission can be found in the words of Rogers and Steinfatt (1999), authors of a popular intercultural communication textbook: "If individuals could attain a higher degree of intercultural competence, they would presumably become better citizens, students, teachers, businesspeople, and so forth. Society would be more peaceful, more productive, and generally a more attractive place to live" (p. 222). In fact, "Individuals would be better able to understand others who are unlike themselves. Through such improved understanding, a great deal of conflict could be avoided; the world would be a better place" (p. 222).[30]

But do our differences—or even our supposed failure to properly manage and navigate our differences—really make strife and conflict between different peoples? Did the slaughter of the Tutsis by the Hutus arise from the differences between these peoples, or even the failure to properly manage and navigate each other's differences? Did the Holocaust arise from the differences between Germans and Jews, or even the failure to properly manage and navigate each other's differences? Did slavery and Jim Crow arise from the differences between Whites and Blacks, or even the failure to properly manage and navigate each other's differences? Did the Rape of Nanking arise from the differences between the Japanese and Chinese, or even the failure to properly manage and navigate each other's differences? We are to assume that by merely attending to the differences that supposedly put us in conflict with each other, all will be well. The origin of this belief can be found at the core of the Western/European worldview,

---

[30] Rogers, E., & Steinfatt, T. M. (1999). *Intercultural communication*. Prospect Heights, IL: Waveland Press.

in us believing that the world is of a natural conflict between opposing forces—in this case, homogeneity versus diversity. Presumably, without favoring and privileging similarity, commonality, and homogeneity, chaos, confusion, and disruption will arise and make communication and civility impossible. Thus intercultural communication insists that all sides abide by a common set of norms and regulations. Enter speech codes and prohibitions against the use of "offensive" and "threatening" language. For the sake of avoiding conflict and disruption so that our society—like a machine—can function smoothly we have no qualms imposing all manner of arbitrary laws and regulations to sustain certain norms of civility and decency.

Yet history makes no case that language diversity threatens stability and social evolution. In fact, the world's most horrendous crimes occurred in places—such as Germany, Yugoslavia, Rwanda, Iraq, Turkey, and Somalia—that had language homogeneity. Nevertheless, even intercultural communication texts and courses have us harboring the fear that without taming and neutralizing and normalizing our differences, chaos and strife will arise. We are never told why our unwillingness to bridge and manage our differences leads inevitably to strife and conflict. We are to simply assume that human diversity must be managed for the good of all. Presumably, without properly accommodating, bridging, and managing our differences, chaos, death, and confusion will arise.

Intercultural communication theory gives us no compelling reason why communication is necessary or even important. It would have us believe that communication can do nothing to alter the threat that human diversity inherently poses. The most we can presumably do is use communication as a tool to tame and navigate our diversity. We are to treat the threat of human diversity as a truth like gravity and the movement of planets. It is outside of us. The most we can supposedly do is find ways to deal with it.

Such are the origins of intercultural communication and what intercultural communication promises to do for us. But the reality is that the threat of human diversity is of our own making. We made this truth. We brought this supposed truth into the world by how we perceive and make sense of the world. Again, to believe that the world is of a conflict between benevolent and malevolent forces is to perceive any kind of diversity suspiciously. That history lends for no case showing human diversity as the origin of us behaving cruelly to each other shows well that our perception of diversity is of our own making. The colonialism in intercultural communication can be found in us now perpetuating this false perception through the global promotion of intercultural communication courses under the guise that they offer vital communication skills for an increasingly global world where multinational organizations are demanding persons with such skills.

Eleven

Criticisms of Metaphors

In shaping how we perceive and relate to things and persons, metaphors are ideological creations—reinforcing and perpetuating what we value and believe. That different worldviews make for different metaphors mean that metaphors are never morally and ideologically neutral. The metaphors of "war" and "machine" are the most dominant metaphors in the Western/European canon. However, these metaphors come with many debilitative consequences.

> ➤ *The war metaphor distorts the consequences of human action.* There is no zero/sum result in war. In reality, war is about degrees of loss—the victor is really the side that loses less. But both sides lose. The metaphor of war masks this reality. It fosters the impression that victory can come without a price. In this way the metaphor of war sanitizes war by downplaying the price that war demands.

> ➤ *The machine metaphor lacks the ability to deal with human complexity, diversity, and ambiguity.* Machines demand conformity and standardization in order to work properly. Every component in a machine must conform to a common set of specifications. There can be no deviation, no disruption, no diversity. Yet all human beings are different and all life systems strive by promoting diversity rather than conformity.

> *The machine metaphor reduces us to components that are measurable and replaceable.* It promotes uniformity and conformity, both of which are contrary to the natural order of the world.

> *The machine metaphor fosters the impression that human problems are to be fixed and solved rather than managed and healed.* For instance, we commonly speak about relationships "breaking down" and the need to "fix" and "repair" our relationships. But relationships in being inherently ecological things can only strive and flourish by changing and evolving. That is, relationships must heal when damaged, and what is involved in healing a relationship is different to what is involved in fixing a relationship.

> *The machine metaphor diminishes our understanding of communication.* In order to function properly, machines need to avoid anything that causes disruption and confusion. This means that standardization is vital for machines to function properly. Although all the components in a machine are different and perform different roles, all must abide by a common set of standards in order for the machine to work properly. In a machine standardization trumps diversity. Diversity means friction and disruption. The influence of the machine metaphor can be seen in our fear of language diversity and our insistence that all persons in the United States speak English. We associate this diversity with strife and disunity. Language diversity will supposedly make for the disintegration of the United States. The machine metaphor can also seen in our viewing of communication competency in terms of avoiding friction and disruption, and thereby saving communication from *"breaking down."* Communication is presumably about agreement. We must be ready to compromise our diversity for the sake of achieving and maintaining communication. However, tension, conflict, and disagreement are integral to communication. Or, put differently, there can

be no communication without tension, conflict, and disagreement, the reason being that all human beings are of different experiences. We each view the world differently, which means that our meanings and understandings will always be different. Removing this diversity from communication is impossible. In fact, this diversity vitalizes communication. It pushes us to forge new meanings and understandings as other meanings and understandings collide with our current meanings and understandings. Without human diversity, communication would have no impetus, no reason for being. That disagreement is inevitable in no way means that disagreement is trouble. Disagreement can be a catalyst. It can be an opportunity to look at something anew. There is also no need for agreement in communication. Instead, communication merely requires a willingness to look at something anew, to be open to the possibility of a different meaning and understanding. Communication is a process of mind. Or, simply put, communication begins with our minds. Our minds shape what we are ultimately capable of meaning and understanding, sharing and interpreting, being and becoming. Our minds also shape how we use and experience language. The machine metaphor diminishes our view of communication by downplaying the power of our minds. It reduces the mind to processes of regulation and calculation. The mind is that which controls a machine's regulation. It resides in a machine's regulator. However, the human mind is capable of doing much more than regulating and calculating. It can create and imagine. It can function beyond the bounds of symbols and language. It can bring new worlds into being. Indeed, standardization impedes our minds by robbing them of the challenges that come with human diversity. Great minds create new meanings that enlarge our sense of possibility.

Twelve

An Epistemology of Conquest

Although worldviews are always in flux as result of encountering and navigating other worldviews, the epistemology that guides the Western/European worldview generally begins on the belief (ontology) that the world is constituted by forces acting upon matter. This remains the foundation of Physics—the study of forces acting on matter.

This belief makes for an epistemology that is committed to understanding how different kinds of forces act upon different kinds of matter, and manipulating this equation for our own survival and prosperity. This epistemological quest—to produce a knowledge that will allow us to control the biological, material, physical, and meteorological realms of the world —pervades every dimension of our society. What emerges is a knowledge that is all about conquest and perceives problems in terms of conquest. Consequently, metaphors of war and machines have laden the language of this epistemology, as well as our understanding of our problems (e.g, The War On Drugs, The War On Poverty, The War On Cancer, The War On Obesity, The War On Gangs, The War On Terror).

I.   Metaphors of War and Machines in Farming.

Machines Now

The recent signing by President Benigno Aquino of the Farm Mechanization Law . . . shows that the [Philippines'] government will continue to prioritize mechanizing farms in the next years to come.

Rex Bingabing, executive director of the Philippine Center for Postharvest Development and Mechanization (PhilMech), the agency under the DA tasked to develop and disperse farm mechanization technologies, said that mechanization can help attract more young people to farming, and more farmers are becoming interested in mechanization.

"Most young people are interested in new technologies and modern innovations. Most are also looking for work that are less labor intensive," he said.

He said that by mechanizing farm work, drudgery could be greatly reduced, which would make farming more attractive to the youth.

"Many had preferred taking training in construction works like welding or metal fabrication. But if they will realize that [farm] mechanization would take away drudgery and increase their productivity, they [young people] would be encouraged to engage in farming operations," Bingabing added.

"Those who are doing the traditional [more on manual] farming are all over 40. The younger ones are usually the operators of four-wheel tractors, combine harvester and transplanters. It seems that it's harder to convince older people to adopt modern technologies. Young people are more open to innovations," Bingabing said.

The mechanization of farm operations can increase production by five percent and reduce postharvest losses to five percent to 10 percent, or even lower. Postharvest losses in Philippine farms is about 15 percent to 20 percent.

In the mid 1990s, an official government survey showed that the farm mechanization level in the Philippines was only 0.52 hp/ha.

Bingabing attributed the increase in the farm mechanization figures to the increase in the uptake of farm machinery by farmers and farmers' groups during the past three years.

"Every time we go around the country for field inspections, the farmers are the ones asking how to avail of the machineries. In the coming years, there would be a lot of farmers acquiring machineries," Bingabing said.

A study on farm mechanization trends in Asia that was completed in 2010 stated that agriculture mechanization is inevitable in the region, and the Philippines has no choice but to catch up to secure its food needs.

In the case of the Philippines, the study stated that "[Agricultural] mechanization level in the field crops sector is still in the developing stage."

For the whole of Asia, the authors said that mechanization can usher in a second "green revolution" in the region's agriculture sector.

"Now, as the region aims for more balanced economic growth, it needs a second, more knowledge-intensive green revolution that combines advances in science and agricultural engineering with the region's unique traditional knowledge to make agriculture more environmentally resilient," it added.

The study showed that in countries where farm mechanization level is high, the "agricultural labor intensity" is conversely low. Agricultural labor intensity indicates the number of workers in a hectare of farmland.

South Korea, which has been self-sufficient in rice and exports various farm products, has an agricultural labor intensity figure of 1.11. While no figure for agricultural labor intensity was given for the Philippines, the figure for Bangladesh, which is also in the developing stages of farm mechanization, was 4.69.

While a reduction in the number of laborers can happen once farm mechanization level increases, the workers at the fields usually benefit from improved conditions.

"Agricultural mechanization plays an increasingly important role in agricultural production in the Asia-Pacific region. It reduces drudgery, increases the safety and comfort of the working environment; it enhances productivity, cropping intensity and production. It increases income for agricultural workers and then improves social equality and overall living standards," the study said.[31]

II. Metaphors of War and Machines in Animals and Plants.

Food For The Future

Corn that is genetically modified to include a natural insecticide, cotton that has been engineered to tolerate herbicides—if you've been reading about such new transgenic crops, you may be asking yourself, "Why do we need this stuff?" After all, American farmers already turn out plenty of high-quality food at low prices.

---

[31] Excerpted from Cariño, C. M. (2013, June 22). The potential of mechanization in agriculture. *The Manila Times.* http://manilatimes.net/the-potential-of-mechanization-in-agriculture/12160/

Yes, it's true that most genetically modified crops now available are barely distinguishable from what they supplant, and so far they have not led to such promised advances as big reductions in the need for agricultural chemicals. And while there is no evidence that genetically engineered crops in the field have caused any harm to human health or done any damage to the environment, planting them obviously entails a risk of unwanted ecological effects.

So shouldn't the genetic engineering of crops be stopped? That is what many critics, here and in Europe, are saying. And if the current generation of crops were all that the genetic engineering of agriculture would produce, that view would be correct, because the risks, while small, would outweigh the benefits.

But the important thing to keep in mind is that the transgenic crops in the news today are just the first manifestations of a fundamental new idea. Much better versions are coming.

For example, the Rockefeller Foundation is sponsoring research on so-called golden rice, a crop designed to improve nutrition in the developing world. Breeders of golden rice are using genetics to build into the rice forms of vitamin A that the body can absorb; vitamin A deficiency is a common problem in poor countries. A second phase of the project will increase the iron content in rice to combat anemia, which is a widespread problem among women in underdeveloped countries.

Golden rice, expected to be for sale in Asia in as little as five years, may offer dramatic improvements in nutrition and health for millions of people, at just shy of zero cost to farmers and consumers.

Similar initiatives using genetic manipulation are aimed at making crops more productive by reducing their dependence on pesticides, fertilizers and irrigation, or by increasing their resistance to plant diseases. Other projects hope to solve problems like peanut allergies by removing the genes for allergens from the plants.

Today 800 million people in poor nations are chronically undernourished, according to the United Nations, and the populations of these countries are expected to grow by an additional two billion to three billion people before the global population peaks sometime in the next century. Merely changing the way food is distributed cannot solve the need for increased agricultural output. But the second and third generations of genetically engineered crops might.

Then there are the health care possibilities. For example, the standard three-shot course required for hepatitis B inoculations in the United States typically costs about $200. There is no way most people in poor nations can afford that, a reason hepatitis B is exacting a terrible toll in Africa. But researchers at Cornell University are working to transfer the genetic code for the hepatitis B vaccine into bananas. If they are successful, hepatitis B inoculations could cost as little as 10 cents per dose and would require no medical personnel to administer them.

This project is one reason that while skeptics in the West are looking askance at genetic engineering, the World Health Organization is having a major conference this month in Geneva to see how this technology can help improve global health.

Of course, the genetic engineering of crops must be carefully regulated. A new system of independent testing and federal oversight might be required, replacing the current hodgepodge in which the Environmental Protection Agency, the Food and Drug Administration and the Department of Agriculture have overlapping and conflicting responsibilities.

But it would be a mistake if the underwhelming results of the first generation of transgenic crops led to laws or boycotts that blocked the second and third generations. After all, it is the world's poorest people who would have the most to lose.[32]

---

[32] Excerpted from Easterbrook, G. (1999, November 19). Food for the future. *New York Times.* http://www.nytimes.com/1999/11/19/opinion/food-for-the-future. html?pagewanted=print

Metaphors matter. As Lera Boroditsky and Paul Thibodeau note, *"Far from being mere rhetorical flourishes, metaphors have profound influences on how we conceptualize and act with respect to important societal issues."* This can be amply seen in a study that both conducted to look at how different metaphors shape our framing of crime. Boroditsky and Thibodeau found that *"participants who read that crime was a beast were about 20 percent more likely to suggest an enforcement-based solution than participants who read that crime was a virus, regardless of their political persuasion."* According to Boroditsky, *"We can't talk about any complex situation – like crime – without using metaphors. Metaphors aren't just used for flowery speech. They shape the conversation for things we're trying to explain and figure out. And they have consequences for determining what we decide is the right approach to solving problems."* In a number of experiments, *"test subjects were asked to read short paragraphs about rising crime rates in the fictional city of Addison and answer questions about the city. The researchers gauged how people answered these questions in light of how crime was described – as a beast or a virus."*

Boroditsky and Thibodeau also found that *"test subjects' proposed solutions differed a great deal depending on the metaphor they were exposed to. In one study, 71 percent of the participants called for more enforcement when they read: "Crime is a beast ravaging the city of Addison."* That number dropped to 54 percent among participants who read an alternative framing: *"Crime is a virus ravaging the city of Addison."* According to Boroditsky, *"People like to think they're objective and making decisions based on numbers. They want to believe they're logical. But they're really being swayed by metaphors."* Indeed, Boroditsky and Thibodeau found that *"Participants who read that crime was a beast were about 20 percent more likely to suggest an enforcement-based solution than participants who read that crime was a virus, regardless of their political persuasion."*[33]

---

[33] Excerpted from Adam Gorlick, A. (2011, February 23). Is crime a virus or a beast? When describing crime, Stanford study shows the word you pick can frame the debate on how to fight it. *Stanford Report.* http://news.stanford.edu/news/2011/february/metaphors-crime-study-022311.html?view=print

Thirteen

Literacy, Texts, & Writing

Machines are making communication increasingly textual—emailing, texting, tweeting, facebooking—and this textual trend is fundamentally changing our society and humanity.

Colonialism has a lot to do with the privileging and promoting of textuality (the written word) over orality (the spoken word).

- Texts allow for domination and conquest—passports (immigration), birth certificates, and identity cards allow us to control the movement of people.

- Texts allow for mass organization and bureaucracy—transcripts, class papers, rosters, change of grade forms, petition forms, examinations, evaluations, and certificates allow for the mass organization of human beings.

- Texts allow for mass production and consumption—orders, contracts, and paper currency make mass production and consumption possible.

- Texts allow for mass indoctrination—the media, the school system, and the church all depend on the publication of texts that will make for the easy and even distribution of certain kinds of information.

- Texts make for superior kinds of surveillance—that our communication is increasingly in the form of texts allows governments to monitor our communication.

Fourteen

Orality and the Spoken Word

We privilege the written word in the Western/European world. We value books and promote the reading, writing, and studying of books. We believe the measure of a civilization can be found in how many books that civilization has produced. We believe that the written word allows a civilization to accumulate knowledge and disseminate this knowledge efficiently and effectively. From a Western/European standpoint, these processes make for progress. This is why many persons view quantity of books as a reliable measure of the progress of a civilization. We also believe that the written word makes for a superior knowledge, one that can be reliably shared and openly critiqued, revised, and refuted. The written word supposedly makes knowledge democratic. It increases who can access our increasing stockpiles of knowledge, and also who can participate in analyzing and contributing to this knowledge. Thus from a Western/European standpoint, the written word constitutes moral, social, and epistemological progress.

However, what to make of the fact that neither Jesus Christ, Muhammad, Siddhartha, Arjuna, nor any other major prophet never left any of the world's most important teachings in writing? As Thomas Merton (1970) notes, "The Bible was originally a body of oral traditions meant to be *recited and listened to in a group especially attuned to its message.* The Bible is not primarily a written or printed text to be scrutinized in private, in a scholar's study or a contemplative cell. It is a body of oral messages, announcements, prophecies, promulgations, recitals, histories, songs of praise, lamentations, etc., which are meant to be read aloud, or chanted, or sung, or recited *in a community convoked for the purpose of a living celebration.* Such a convocation is a synagogue or church (ekklesia—community of those called to hear and respond" (p. 44).[34] Thus, if the written word is so obviously superior to the spoken word, as the Western/European world generally assumes, why did all these prophets entrust these knowledges to the spoken word? The fact is that the spoken word (orality) has many distinct attributes.

Attributes of The Spoken Word

➢ Orality promotes integrity and character. In many cultures a person's word is assumed to be sacred. In most oral-based cultures giving your word obligates you to keep your word, regardless of the consequences that come with doing so. Thus people are comfortable making contracts and all manner of agreements through the spoken word because one's word is seen as a reflection of one's integrity and character.

➢ Orality promotes restraint. In many cultures the spoken word is assumed to have either negative and positive power, such as the power to either harm or heal. Thus words should always be used carefully and with restraint.

➢ Orality allows for mobility. The spoken word lends for a knowledge that cannot be stopped at borders and confiscated. In this way, orality allows for knowledge to move freely from place to place.

➢ Orality impedes the ability of governments to monitor our communication by leaving no record of our communication.

---

[34] Merton, T. (1970). *Opening the Bible.* Collegeville, MN: Liturgical Press.

➢ Orality undermines domination and conquest. Through the written word governments can control populations by creating documents (e.g., birth certificates, passports, ID cards, contracts, currency) that control the movement and behaviors of various populations. The spoken word undermines such control.

➢ Orality promotes equality and diversity. When knowledge resides in books, laws can be passed to prohibit the reading of certain books that are judged to be a threat to the status quo, making access to the knowledge in these books nearly impossible to acquire. The spoken word undermines that kind of control of knowledge. There is simply no way for any government to know and even track what knowledge resides within any person or community.

Fifteen

Criticisms of Textuality

Many civilizations do have both textual and oral traditions. Textuality refers to the hegemony of the written, or the belief that the written word makes for a superior civilization by making for a superior knowledge. But there are criticisms of textuality that should be noted.

➤ Textuality impedes our psychological, relational, communicational, and spiritual development in terms of promoting isolation and alienation. It undermines our ability to face each other openly and honestly. Indeed, being afraid to openly and publicly speak our truths makes for many kinds of neuroses and psychoses.

➤ Textuality blocks our psychological, relational, communicational, and spiritual development by encouraging us to focus on the interior rather than the exterior—resulting in an obsession to know a person's intention and motivation. Yet in the end what really matters are our actions and decisions rather than our intentions and motivations.

➤ Textuality blocks our psychological, relational, communicational, and spiritual development by encouraging us to hold on the past thereby compromising the power of the present.

Indeed, texts are often difficult to dispose of, and thus have a way of hanging around and compromising the present.

➢ Textuality blocks our psychological, relational, communicational, and spiritual development by promoting conformity—e.g., syllabuses, manuals, curriculums, handbooks, and so forth. Written rules and regulations block flexibility, diversity, and spontaneity.

➢ Textuality promotes abstractions and arbitrary categorizations. It divorces us from reality and leaves us in a world of abstractions. Textuality discourages us from dealing with reality on its own terms by encouraging us to use language correctly and strategically rather than honestly and courageously. We find this abstraction in our many euphemisms—"contractors" rather than "mercenaries", "enhanced interrogation techniques" rather than "torture", "surgical strike" rather than "bombing."

➢ Textuality impedes situational thinking. That is, textuality blocks us from dealing with reality on its own terms. Often, reality refuses to fit neatly into our words, concepts, and schemes. Yet reality must still be dealt with, meaning that problems must still be managed and obstacles navigated for the sake of moving on.

Sixteen

Arguments for Orality

Besides making for different ideological structures and reflecting different epistemological foundations, the written and spoken also make for different psychological structures. In *Orality and Literacy*, Walter Ong highlights these differences.

> *Oral cultures tend to be devoid of cognitive structures that promote geometrical figures, abstract categorization, formal logical reasoning processes, definitions, comprehensive descriptions, and articulated self analysis (p. 54).*

> *Writing fosters abstractions that disengage knowledge from the [environment] where human beings struggle with one another. It separates the knower and known. On the other hand, by keeping knowledge embedded in the life world, orality situates knowledge within a context of struggle (p. 43).*

> *Primary orality fosters personality structures that in certain ways are more communal and externalized, and less introspective than those common among literates. Oral communication unites people in groups. Writing and reading are solitary activities that throw the psyche back on itself (p. 68).*

Persons whose worldview has been formed by high literacy need to remind themselves that in functionally oral cultures the past is not felt as . . . terrain, laden with verifiable facts and bits of information. It is the domain of the ancestors, a resource for renewing awareness of present existence. . . . Orality knows no lists or charts or figures.[35]

---

[35] Excerpts from Walter Ong's (1982) *Literacy And Orality*. New York: Routledge.

Seventeen

Colonization, Quantification & Communication

Most oral-based civilizations have now been erased, marginalized, or colonized by writing-based civilizations. The Western/European world continues to be responsible for a lot of this colonization. Textuality represents the hegemony of the written word, or the belief that the written word—either in the form of words or numbers—is superior to all others. This hegemony can be found in our belief that numbers—and all the methodologies that use numbers—make for the most reliable and valuable kind of knowledge.

Numbers are presumably devoid of biases and prejudices. Race, ethnicity, nationality, gender, and sexual orientation can do nothing to change the fact that two plus two is four. Nor do numbers have any regard for politics. Two plus two is four in any space or place. Numbers are presumably objective and capable of correcting for our supposed flaws and weaknesses, such as our biases and prejudices. For instance, Paul Dirac, a Physics Nobel Laureate, said, as Galileo also said, *"that mathematics is the language that nature speaks. When expressed in mathematical equations, the laws of quantum mechanics are clear and unambiguous. Confusion arises from misguided attempts to translate the laws from mathematics to human language. Human language describes the world of everyday life, and lacks the concepts that could describe quantum processes accurately.*"[36]

We assume numbers make for a superior knowledge that ultimately makes for a superior civilization. Consequently, mathematics is an integral component in our educational system and a command of mathematics is seen as a reflection of a superior mind.

Communication studies abides by these beliefs. Numbers play an integral role in communication studies.

---

[36] Dyson, F. (2010, February 25). Silent quantum genius. *NY Review of Books.*

Eighteen

Assumptions in Quantitative Research

N umbers are the foundation of quantitative research, which guides most of the research in communication studies. The primary assumption in quantitative research is that human behavior is quantifiable, measureable, and observable. The challenge is merely to find the methodologies that will make this so. In this way, quantitative research requires that communication be defined and understood in ways that lend for observation, categorization, classification, and quantification. By believing (ontology) that human behavior is quantifiable, measureable, and observable, communication becomes something that is also quantifiable, measureable, and observable (epistemology). As always, how we define something will shape how we perceive and make sense of something, just as much as how we perceive and make sense of something will shape how we define that something.

Viewing communication as a quantifiable, measureable, and observable phenomenon begins with viewing communication as a linguistic and symbolic process. Simply put, communication is presumably a process that fundamentally involves language and symbols—things that are observable and quantifiable. We divide communication into verbal and nonverbal communication. We further divide verbal communication into different kinds of communication (e.g., persuasive messages, informative messages, supportive messages) and nonverbal communication into different kinds of communication (e.g., kinesics, proxemics, haptics, oculesics, chronemics). Our goal is to make communication amenable to different kinds of quantitative analyses by generating as many observable variables as possible that could be measured, compared, and evaluated. We assume that these kinds of quantitative analyses will make for a rigorous knowledge of communication.

Ultimately, the definition of communication that pervades communication studies assumes that human behavior is quantifiable, measureable, and observable. This can be seen in the official definition that the National Communication Association, which "advances communication as the discipline that studies all forms, modes, media and consequences of communication through humanistic, social scientific and aesthetic inquiry," officially forwards.

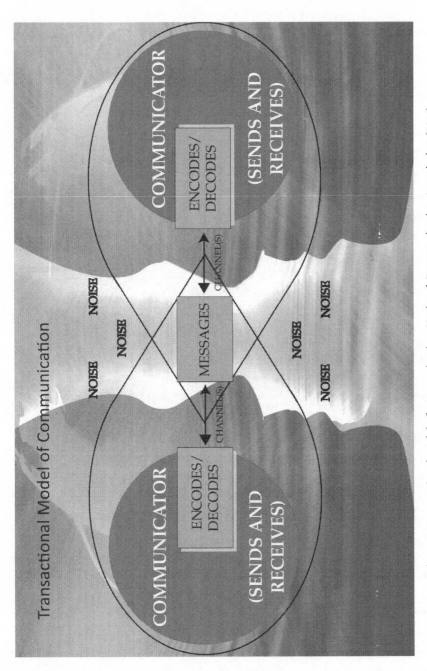

Figure 1. Transactional model of communication, National Communication Association (2014).

What is Communication?

The discipline of communication focuses on how people use messages to generate meanings within and across various contexts, cultures, channels, and media. The discipline promotes the effective and ethical practice of human communication.

Communication is a diverse discipline which includes inquiry by social scientists, humanists, and critical and cultural studies scholars. A body of scholarship and theory, about all forms of human communication, is presented and explained in textbooks, electronic publications, and academic journals. In the journals, researchers report the results of studies that are the basis for an ever-expanding understanding of how we all communicate.

Transactional Model Of Communication

The transactional model of communication is a graphic representation of the collaborative and ongoing message exchange between individuals, or an individual and a group of individuals, with the goal of understanding each other. A communicator encodes (e.g., puts thoughts into words and gestures), then transmits the message via a channel (e.g., speaking, email, text message) to the other communicator(s) who then decode the message (e.g., take the words and apply meaning to them). The message may encounter noise (e.g., any physical, psychological, or physiological distraction or interference), which could prevent the message from being received or fully understood as the sender intended.

Areas within Communication

Areas of emphasis differ from one institution to another, but listed below are some of the most common areas of study:

Applied Communication - The study of how communication theory, research, and/or best practices help inform knowledge and theory about communication for practical issues.

Communication Education - The study of communication in the classroom and other pedagogical contexts.

Communication Theory - The study of principles that account for the impact of communication in human social interaction.

Electronic Media - The study of radio, television, media technology, and web design with streaming audio and video.

Health Communication - The study of communication as it relates to health professionals and health education, including the study of provider-client interaction, as well as the diffusion of health information through public health campaigns.

International and Intercultural Communication - The study of communication among individuals of different cultural backgrounds, including the study of similarities and differences across cultures.

Interpersonal Communication - The study of communication behaviors in dyads (pairs) and their impact on personal relationships.

Language and Social Interaction - The study of the structure of verbal and nonverbal behaviors occurring in social interaction.

Legal Communication - The study of the role of communication as it relates to the legal system.

Mass Communication and Media Literacy - The study of how mass forms of communication, such as print, radio and television disseminate information and influence society.

Mediation and Dispute Resolution - The study of understanding, management, and resolution of conflict within intrapersonal, interpersonal, and intergroup situations.

Organizational Communication - The study of processes used to analyze communication needs of organizations and social interaction, including how to improve communication between supervisors and employees.

Performance Studies - The study of components such as performer(s), text, audience, and context within the communication discipline.

Political Communication - The study of the role that communication plays in political systems.

Public Address - The study of speakers and speeches, including the historical and social context of platforms, campaigns, and movements.

Public Relations - The study of the management of communication between an organization and its audiences.

Rhetorical Criticism - The process of defining, classifying, analyzing, interpreting, and/or evaluating rhetorical artifacts.

Semiotics - The use of verbal and nonverbal symbols and signs in human communication.

Small Group Communication - The study of communication systems among three or more individuals who interact around a common purpose and who influence one another.

Speech Communication - The study of the nature, processes, and effects of human symbolic interaction. While speech is the most obvious mode of communication, human symbolic interaction includes a variety of verbal and nonverbal codes.

Theatre and Drama - The study and production of dramatic literature.

Visual Communication - The study of visual data, such as architecture, photography, visual art, advertising, film, and television as it relates to communication.[37]

The National Communication Association (NCA) is the largest body of communication scholars, teachers, and students in the world. It *"advances communication as the discipline that studies all forms, modes, media and consequences of communication through humanistic, social scientific and aesthetic inquiry. The NCA serves the scholars, teachers, and practitioners who are its members by enabling and supporting their professional interests in research and teaching. Dedicated to fostering and promoting free and ethical communication, the NCA promotes the widespread appreciation of the importance of communication in public and private life, the application of competent communication to improve the quality of human life and relationships, and the use of knowledge about communication to solve human problems."* Thus when the NCA declares that communication is a transactional process involving linguistic and symbolic codes, this definition comes with enormous political and institutional backing. To call this definition into question is to call the mission of the association into question as the mission speaks to what communication can potentially do. This begins with how communication is defined and also who is defining communication.

---

[37] What is Communication? http://www.natcom.org/discipline/

Nineteen

Methods in Quantitative Research

A n epistemology has various means of acquiring what it defines as knowledge. We refer to these means as methodologies. Only the knowledge derived from these methodologies is assumed to be legitimate, which again reminds us that our methodologies reinforce what we believe and define as knowledge. Indeed, no methodology can produce a knowledge that is contrary to the epistemology that brings that methodology into the world. A methodology serves an epistemology by acquiring only the knowledge that serves the interest of that epistemology.

A variety of methodologies fall under the heading of quantitative research in communication studies.

I. Experiment research in communication studies often involves studying the effects of different kinds of messages on different populations and conditions to identify either causal or correlational relationships.

Effects of Teacher Clarity and Nonverbal Immediacy on Student Learning, Receiver Apprehension, and Affect
Joseph L. Chesebro
Abstract
This study examined the role that nonverbal immediacy plays in clear teaching, as well as the effects clear and immediate teaching

have on student learning, state receiver apprehension, and affect. The results indicate that clarity, as defined in this study, is an important factor in student learning, receiver apprehension, and affect. Students who were taught by a clear teacher learned more than those who were taught by an unclear teacher, experienced less state receiver apprehension, and had more positive affect for the instructor and the course material.

II. Survey research in communication studies usually involves the use of surveys to discover the impact of various messages that respondents were exposed to.

College Students' Attributions of Teacher Misbehaviors

Dawn M. Kelsey, Patricia Kearney, Timothy G. Plax, Terre H. Allen.

Abstract

Grounded in attribution theory, this investigation examined explanations students provide when college teachers misbehave, and the influence of perceived teacher immediacy shaping those interpretations. Across two different samples, college students responded to questionnaires assessing perceptions of their teachers' immediacy, teacher misbehaviors, and attributions of misbehavior consistency and causality. Results . . . revealed that students recognize teacher misbehaviors and apply an interpretive framework in which they view the teacher . . . as the primary cause of teacher misbehaviors.

III. Network analysis in communication studies involves systematically mapping and measuring the direction and movement of communication messages within a system.

Network Structure in Virtual Organizations

Manju K. Ahuja and Kathleen M. Carley, Florida State University and Carnegie Mellon University

Abstract

Virtual organizations that use email to communicate and coordinate their work toward a common goal are becoming ubiquitous.

However, little is known about how these organizations work. Much prior research suggests that virtual organizations, for the most part because they use information technology to communicate, will be decentralized and non-hierarchical. This paper examines the behavior of one such organization. The analysis is based on a case study of the communication structure and content of communications among members of a virtual organization during a four-month period. We empirically measure the structure of a virtual organization and find evidence of hierarchy. The findings imply that the communication structure of a virtual organization may exhibit different properties on different dimensions of structure. We also examine the relationship among task routineness, organizational structure, and performance. Results indicate that the fit between structure and task routineness affects the perception of performance, but may not affect the actual performance of the organization. Thus, this virtual organization is similar to traditional organizations in some ways and dissimilar in other ways. It was similar to traditional organizations in so far as task-structure fit predicted perceived performance. However, it was dissimilar to traditional organizations in so far as fit did not predict objective performance. To the extent that the virtual organizations may be similar to traditional organizations, existing theories can be expanded to study the structure and perceived performance of virtual organizations. New theories may need to be developed to explain objective performance in virtual organizations

In experiment research, survey research, or network analysis research, the goal is to discover patterns and relationships that reflect the behaviors of persons in a population. Quantitative research assumes that all populations are already laden with noteworthy patterns and relationships as human beings tend to be shaped by the same biological and psychological forces and motives. In quantitative research the goal is to discover these patterns and relationships—that is, the patterns and relationships that are assumed to be shared.

This is why quantitative research is comfortable making bold hypotheses and predictions with high degrees of certainty. As regards the human experience, quantitative research assumes and promotes commonality. Without the assumption of commonality, quantitative research would be impossible. It is commonality that presumably makes the findings of quantitative research generalizable and also for the making of covering laws and principles. In quantitative research these are good things. These are the things that make for public policy. In this way, quantitative research methods work insidiously to reinforce a Western/European worldview that values commonality and a suspicion of diversity.

Twenty

Criticisms of Quantitative Research Methods

As much as quantitative research provides most of the methods used in communication investigations, there are criticisms of quantitative research that need to be noted.

> ➤ Quantitative research aspires to remove any force that could interfere with our arriving at a definitive relationship between our selected variables. For instance, any study exploring the relationship between mood and persuasion must control for any force—such as age, race, culture, religion—that could undermine our understanding of this relationship. But this is all but impossible to do, as no human being can know all the forces that could possibly affect the relationship between mood and persuasion. Thus the ability to make any kind of definitive claim about the relationship between mood and persuasion is impossible.

> ➤ Quantitative research assumes and promotes detachment— separation between object and subject, knower and known, thought and feeling. But this detachment is illusory. Those who are conducting the study are always influencing the behaviors of those in the study by simply putting those persons under study and in conditions determined by those doing the study.

Also, those under study must follow only the instructions set by those conducting the study (e.g., "check the box that best captures your reaction to the following messages").

➤ Quantitative research promotes abstraction by promoting modeling. That is, in aiming to produce neat and tidy models that presumably represent reality, quantitative research must make reality seem neat and tidy. This usually involves distorting reality.

Winning The Nobel Prize

Again, as in his [Paul Krugman, Nobel Laureate in Economics] trade theory, it was not so much his idea that was significant as the translation of the idea into mathematical language. "I explained this basic idea"—of economic geography—"to a non-economist friend," Krugman wrote, "who replied in some dismay, 'Isn't that pretty obvious?' And of course it is." Yet, because it had not been well modelled, the idea had been disregarded by economists for years. Krugman began to realize that in the previous few decades economic knowledge that had not been translated into models had been effectively lost, because economists didn't know what to do with it.

Krugman . . . could take an intriguing notion that had come up in real-world discussions, pare away the details (knowing just what to take out and what was essential), and refine what was left into a clean, clever, "cute" (as he liked to put it), and simple model. "It's poetry," Kenneth Rogoff, an economist at Harvard, says. "I mean, you go back to his first book and there was this beautiful chart about what the Volcker contraction did to output that swept aside so much—he just drew this little graph which really cleared the air. I've heard economists use the word 'poet' in describing him for decades."

Krugman's theories of trade and economic geography are still taught everywhere. "I think there's a pretty good case to be made that the stuff that I stressed in the models is a less important story than the things that I left out because I couldn't model them, like spillovers of information and social networks," he says. But failure to represent reality accurately is rarely a fatal flaw in an economics model—what's valued is the model's usefulness as an analytic tool. The most successful paper Krugman ever wrote was about target zones, and it was completely wrong. "Empirically, it doesn't work at all," Krugman says. "People loved it as an academic thing, but it had some very strong predictions about interest rates inside target zones. Those predictions all turned out to be wrong. But nobody attacked me for that. I was showing that if target zones worked the way that people say they're supposed to work, then this is how it would play out."[38]

➢ Quantitative research values objectivity—removing or limiting our biases and prejudices. But objectivity is impossible to attain. To be human is to have biases and prejudices. We are always understanding the world from a cultural, historical, and epistemological standpoint. No human being falls out of the sky. We have experiences, and our experiences shape our view of things and our ways of dealing with things.

➢ Quantitative research perpetuates a definition of communication that downplays the complexity of the human condition. We are capable of relating and understanding each other without language and symbols. Indeed, by defining communication as a linguistic and symbolic phenomenon, quantitative research perpetuates the view that communication is about what is spoken, written, and symbolized. This is supposedly what is important, and communication curriculums put the focus on helping us use language and symbols properly and effectively. Being eloquent and coherent is a measure of communication success. But communication is also about what

---

[38] Excerpted and adapted from MacFarquhar, L. The deflationist. *New Yorker*. http://www.newyorker.com/reporting/2010/03/01/100301fa_fact_macfarquhar?currentPage=7#ixzz0h2Ycj8UV

is never spoken, written, and symbolized—such as what is deliberately omitted, concealed, and silenced. Indeed, what is unspoken is often much more important than what is spoken, written, and symbolized. In fact, many cultures believe that what is unspoken is more important than what is spoken, and thus cultivate a command of the unspoken word. The problem is that quantitative research has no way of quantifying this unspoken dimension of communication. It is unquantifiable because it is unobservable.

> Quantitative research discourages the probing of many important questions—that is, questions that will never lend for numbers. What is the meaning of life? What is the purpose of life? Why do human beings believe? As Albert Einstein once said, *"not everything that can be counted counts, and not everything that counts can be counted."*

> Quantitative research diminishes human diversity. It reduces human diversity to only that which is observable, quantifiable, and measurable. Simply put, quantitative research reduces human diversity to boxes, reinforcing the view that human diversity can fit neatly into boxes.

> Quantitative research mistakes knowledge for wisdom. The goal of quantitative research is to produce, accumulate, and disseminate knowledge. These processes supposedly promote our prosperity. But being wise is different to being knowledgeable. We can have many communication degrees and still have problems sharing our thoughts.

> Quantitative research devalues methods that defy the limits of numbers, such as walking, meditating, dreaming, and praying. Yet quantitative research can make no case that such methodologies have no value. After all, quantitative research has no way of studying these things to begin with.

> Quantitative research values deduction and the making of universal laws and principles. Deduction is about moving from the universal to the local. Quantitative research arrives at deduction through induction, building from one study and replicating findings until all the findings become consistent. Yet quantitative research has a poor record of replicating results and findings. In fact, consistent findings are rarely achieved. The reason being that regardless of our best efforts, every human being is different and thereby every group under study is different.

When Findings Disappear

Before the effectiveness of a drug can be confirmed, it must be tested and tested again. Different scientists in different labs need to repeat the protocols and publish their results. The test of replicability, as it's known, is the foundation of modern research. Replicability is how the community enforces itself. It's a safeguard for the creep of subjectivity. Most of the time, scientists know what results they want, and that can influence the results they get. The premise of replicability is that the scientific community can correct for these flaws.

But now all sorts of well-established, multiply confirmed findings have started to look increasingly uncertain. It's as if our facts were losing their truth: claims that have been enshrined in textbooks are suddenly unprovable. This phenomenon doesn't yet have an official name, but it's occurring across a wide range of fields, from psychology to ecology. In the field of medicine, the phenomenon seems extremely widespread, affecting not only antipsychotics but also therapies ranging from cardiac stents to Vitamin E and antidepressants.

For many scientists, the effect is especially troubling because of what it exposes about the scientific process. If replication is what separates the rigor of science from the squishiness of pseudoscience, where do we put all these rigorously validated findings that can no longer be proved? Which results should we believe? Francis Bacon, the early-modern philosopher and pioneer of the scientific method, once declared that experiments were essential, because they allowed us to "put nature to the question." But it appears that nature often gives us different answers.[39]

> Quantitative research values pieces rather than wholes. As seen in communication research, qualitative research is always trying to reduce communication into many variables as possible. But separation, division, and fragmentation remove all the complexity that makes for communication. Context is most important in determining what a human being means, and context cannot be reduced, categorized, nor quantified. All contexts are fluid and different.

---

[39] Excerpted from Lehrer, J. (2010, December 13). The truth wears off: Is there something wrong with the scientific method? *New Yorker.* http://www.newyorker.com/ reporting/2010/12/13/101213fa_fact_lehrer?currentPage=1

Twenty One

Implications of Quantification on Communication Studies

Quantitative research needs boxes—*"Check the box that best captures your response to the following questions."* Boxes reduce human beings to variables that are quantifiable, measurable, and observable. Boxes also make for tidy comparisons and lend for statistical analyses. Boxes also allow us to exercise control over our research process by allowing us to manage and organize the identity of our research subjects. Yet the problems with putting human beings into boxes are many.

➤ Boxes are born out of the need to impose order on the world, such as putting different human beings into boxes so as to help manage human diversity. That is, boxes are born purely out of social forces. Understanding the origins of these forces is vital to understanding how boxes are supposed to work and for what purposes.

➤ Boxes diminish our complexity, diversity, mystery, and ultimately our humanity by reducing us to units that can be sorted like oranges and apples. Our complexity and diversity come from the fact that human beings are relational, sexual, spiritual, physical, material, historical, sensual, emotional, existential, ecological, primal, geographical, and cultural beings. Downplaying or missing this complexity and diversity presents serious problems. To begin with, our identity exceeds any one dimension. We could be of the same sexual orientation, but be of fundamentally different social, political, spiritual, material, historical, and cultural persuasions. Also, besides the fact that these different dimensions influence and shape each other, these different dimensions are also inseparable. Thus knowing where one begins and ends is simply impossible. Moreover, downplaying or missing our complexity and diversity tends to make believe that only one dimension is most important to us (such as sexual orientation). But the person of a certain box (in this case sexual orientation) is also a son/daughter, brother/sister, aunt/ uncle, niece/nephew, friend/colleague, Democrat/Republican, communist/capitalist/anarchist, Christian/Buddhist/Hindu/ Atheist, working class/middle class/upper class, and so forth. Persons can be African American, Republican, Christian, and homosexual. Finally, reducing our complexity and diversity reduces the totality of a person's humanity by reducing the person to only one dimension (in this case, sexual orientation) and usually the dimension that matters to others. This process allows for the beginnings of processes that dehumanize and denigrate. A case in point would be reducing peoples to "illegal immigrants" (thus the language of our "illegal immigration problem") and thereby masking the fact that these peoples are also Christians (thus no mention of our "illegal Christian problem").

➤ Boxes promote stereotyping. We are all different in that our many dimensions (social, cultural, historical, material, geographical) will always be different, and thereby we will react to the world differently/deal with the world differently/interpret the world differently/view the world differently. That is, the fact that people check the same box means absolutely nothing. Therefore to say that "this is offensive to black people" is stereotyping as this claim erases the diversity amongst black people.

➢ Boxes perpetuate our fear and suspicion of confusion—such as demanding persons fit neatly into various boxes or simply choose a box.

➢ Boxes promote conformity by attaching certain expectations to different boxes. (e.g., African-Americans are expected to be Democrats, Homosexuals are expected to support gay marriage, Latinos are expected to support immigration, Jews are expected to support Israel)

➢ Boxes promote alienation by keeping us bound to the expectations that come with different boxes. That is, boxes block us from exploring what resides beyond the confines and borders of boxes, meaning that boxes discourage us from exploring various instincts, impulses, and desires.

➢ Finally, boxes impede communication by impeding our own capacity to deal with confusion, resulting in us projecting our own fear of ourselves upon others.

Twenty Two

The Case for
Quantitative Research

H egemony means that most communication departments have curriculums with required methods courses that focus on intro-ducing quantitative research methods and techniques, and making students proficient in these methods and techniques.

Syllabus One

Communication Research Methods

Required Texts
Quantitative Research Methods for Communication, by Jason S. Wrench, Candice Thomas-Maddox, Virginia Peck Richmond, and James C. McCroskey, second edition; published by Oxford University Press, ISBN: 978-0199931804

Publication manual of the American Psychological Association, sixth edition; published by American Psychological Association.

Overview of the Course
This course is designed to do the following:

1. Increase your knowledge of the principles, objectives, and limitations of behavioral and social science research methods.
2. Expose you to the logic of how people studying human communication come to make sense of what they observe.
3. Provide opportunities for you to experience both the research and analysis processes and critique the research that has been done by others in the field.

Course Objectives
By the end of this course, students should be able to:

1. Design and implement research agendas
2. Find and analyze relevant literature for specific research questions
3. Interpret results from research projects
4. Present data, summarize findings and draw conclusions based upon research
5. Analyze data using descriptive and simple statistical tests
6. Prepare a research report and a proposal for future research

Grading and Assignments

QUIZZES (10%): You will take five (5) short quizzes over the course of the semester, each of which will be worth 2% of your final grade.

HOMEWORK ASSIGNMENTS (20%): You will complete ten (10) homework assignments over the course of the semester, each of which will be worth 2% of your final grade.

TESTS (30%): You will take two (2) blue book examinations this semester. Each of these will be open book and open note. As you will be taking these exams in class, your time will necessarily be limited and it will benefit you greatly to prepare ahead of time.

TERM PROJECT (40%): The biggest part of your grade this semester will come from a group project. The goal of this project is to enable you to use the skills that you learn through the course in a useful and concise manner. Since this project is fairly in-depth, your planning will be very important. The term project is broken down into six different phases:

- Phase One: Project Proposal/IRB
- Phase Two: Data Collection
- Phase Three: Literature Review
- Phase Four: Statistical Analysis
- Phase Five: Data Write-Up
- Phase Six: Research Presentation

Syllabus Two

Communication Research Methods

Course Overview

Scientific discovery is one of the most exciting experiences anyone can enjoy. This is especially true in the social sciences, because such important and useful lessons can be learned. To understand how and why people think and act as they do is to create powerful handles for improving the quality of life for us all on earth now and for future generations to follow us.

How can tennis team practices be designed to improve the players' performances? What can children be taught in school that will prevent them from becoming addicted to cigarette smoking? What can a political candidate say and do during a campaign in order to win a presidential election? How should cell phones be designed to most effectively prevent them from causing automobile accidents? How can racism in America be eliminated? Social science can provide answers to all these questions and many more, enabling society to maximize individual happiness and collective life satisfaction.

Speculations abound about the nature and causes of human cognition and behavior, but many of those suspicions turn out to be wrong. Only when our instincts are subjected to objective evaluation using the scientific method can we distinguish illusion from reality.

The purpose of this course is to introduce you to the tools for doing such work. If you are interested in considering a career that entails conducting social science research, these are tools you will find valuable in doing your work. But almost any career involves and benefits from using social science evidence to inform decision-making. This course will teach you how to interpret this evidence and how to differentiate reliable studies from studies you should view skeptically.

To conduct social research investigating any phenomenon of interest to you, you will need to know:

(1) what findings exist in the published literature on your phenomenon,
(2) how to collect objective and accurate data that permit strong scientific inferences,
(3) how to analyze the data you collect to reach appropriate conclusions,
(4) how to interpret your findings and identify their implications,
(5) how to plan your next study of the phenomenon, to build on your last and move your understanding forward even more.

This course will teach you to read research reports to identify the fundamentals of the findings and their meaning. It will expose you to the fundamentals of the primary social science research designs in use these days: laboratory experiments, field experiments, surveys, and unobtrusive methods. It will expose you to the fundamentals of data analysis. And it will expose you to techniques for report writing.

Arguments For Quantitative Research In Communication

✓ *Makes communication research consistent with the tradition and history of quantitative research in other disciplines (e.g., physics, mathematics, biology).*

✓ *By quantifying communication concepts and using statistical procedures for evaluating differences and relationships, communication researchers are able to make precise and exact comparisons (e.g., communication apprehension).*

✓ *Because we can now quantify communication phenomena, we can make comparisons, and those comparisons can be made among a large group of participants.*[40]

---

[40] Keyton, J. *Communication Research: Asking Questions, Finding Answers.* New York: McGraw-Hill.

Twenty Three

Notions Absent in Communication Inquiry and Theory

Quantitative research focuses on only concepts that can be made quantifiable, measurable, and observable. These concepts will come to form the foundation of our knowledge in communication studies. In other words, these are the concepts that will be found in communication textbooks, and will be the subject of communication research and theory development. We will use these concepts to frame and describe our communication behaviors and that of others. We would even use these concepts to make public policy. One such concept is communication apprehension (CA). It was born out of quantitative research. Fear of public speaking is understood in terms of communication apprehension. According to James McCroskey, who is most associated with the development of the concept and also a staunch proponent of quantitative research in communication studies, communication apprehension is the broad term that refers to an individual's *"fear or anxiety associated with either real or anticipated communication with another person or persons."*[41] Communication apprehension is presumably a psychological response to evaluation. This psychological response

---

[41] McCroskey, J. C. (2001). An introduction to rhetorical communication. Boston, MA: Allyn & Bacon.

presumably becomes physical as our body responds to the threat the mind perceives.

Hegemony means that the concepts that form the foundation of our communication knowledge—like communication apprehension—make for a certain kind of reality that reflects and reinforces the worldview that made for the epistemology, that in turn made for the methodologies that brought these concepts into the world.

Hegemony means that notions that are unquantifiable are absent in communication journals and textbooks. These concepts rarely appear in our descriptions of reality and human behavior. There will be no job descriptions for persons who study these concepts. Hegemony also means that persons who value these concepts are on the margins of communication studies. Still, the list of concepts absent in communication studies is striking.

Love
Mercy
Humility
Compassion
Inspiration
Forgiveness
Tenderness
Intuition
Prayer
Visions
Doubt
Faith
Belief
Grace
Space
Place
Spirit
God

This list raises all kinds of questions. How did we come to believe— and continue to assume—that these concepts have no place in our knowledge of communication? What is the value of any knowledge of communication that is devoid of these concepts? Finally, how would the entry of these concepts change our teaching and studying of communication, and how do we need to define communication in order to make for the inclusion of these concepts?

Twenty Four

The Case Against Quantitative Methods in Communication Research

A methodology is only capable of generating the knowledge that the epistemology that brought that methodology into the world defines as knowledge. Simply put, methodologies do the bidding of epistemologies. An epistemology that assumes that knowledge is quantifiable because human processes are quantifiable makes methodologies like experiment research, survey research, and network analysis inevitable. These methodologies are incapable of producing a different kind of knowledge.

So as much as quantitative methodologies will continue to generate vast stockpiles of knowledge, this knowledge will always conform to what our worldview already defines as knowledge. Diversity in knowledge will be impossible, meaning that the ability of epistemologies to create diverse methodologies that will create diverse knowledges is impossible. As much as methodologies do the bidding of epistemologies, epistemologies do the bidding of worldviews and the civilizations that abide by these worldviews. This is how worldviews are self-perpetuating, self-legitimizing, and difficult to disrupt.

We create only the knowledge that conforms to what we believe and are willing to believe. This is the inextricable relationship between epistemology and ontology. Yet this in no way means the knowledge any methodology produces is inherently defective. It merely means that we should concern ourselves with understanding the kind of knowledge the methodology is capable of producing, the purpose of the knowledge, and the value of the knowledge in terms of expanding our sense of what is possible. We can frame these concerns in questions.

For Instance

Do quantitative methods in communication research enrich our understanding of the human experience and what being human means?

Do quantitative methods in communication research deepen our understanding of the world?

Do quantitative methods in communication research help us create a world with less misery and suffering?

Do quantitative methods in communication research help us live more meaningful lives?

Twenty Five

Primary Assumptions in Qualitative Research

The hegemony of the written word (textuality) is found in both quantitative research and qualitative research. Whereas staunch proponents of quantitative research claim that numbers make for a superior knowledge, staunch proponents of qualitative research are equally adamant that words make for a superior knowledge of the human condition.

Most communication research textbooks generally cover both kinds of research and promote the embracing of this supposed methodological diversity. We are advised to select the methodology that best suits the nature of our inquiry. Nevertheless, qualitative research operates on many distinct assumptions.

1) *Human experience is best captured and articulated in language rather than in numbers. Numbers presumably lack the elasticity to capture our complexity, mystery, and ambiguity.*

2) *Those who we are studying and seeking to understand should be allowed to articulate their own experiences and realities in their own words and on their own terms. Doing differently violates the humanity of these persons.*

3) *There is no separation between those doing the studying and those under study. Those doing the studying should acknowledge their presence and all that it means.*

4) *Every reality and/or experience is different because every human being is different. Thus no person's or group's reality is generalizable.*

Twenty Six

Methods in Qualitative Research

The methodologies that form qualitative research take a variety of forms and require different kinds of training.

I. Ethnography. Through immersion, intensive interviewing, and reflexive practice, ethnography aims to understand what are our interpretive schemes and how do such schemes shape and create different ways of experiencing, understanding, and organizing our worlds.

LGBT Pride as a Cultural Protest Tactic in a Southern City
Katherine McFarland Bruce, Wake Forest University.
Abstract
In 2009, Pride came to Dixieville. In this unlikely Southern city, 350 people participated in a Pride march to advocate for improved social conditions for lesbian, gay, bisexual, and transgender (LGBT) citizens. Drawing on ethnographic interviews and observations, I reveal that this march did not fit with the contentious politics model of social movements which defines protest tactics as those that target the state for political/legal change. My findings indicate that the march served primarily as a powerful cultural statement enacted by LGBT community advocates. Guided by Verta Taylor's framework of contestation, intentionality, and

collective identity, I explain why the march participants viewed Pride as the most effective means to advocate for LGBT people despite its dissimilarity with state-targeted tactics. I also demonstrate how Pride answered the specific challenges faced by LGBT people in their city by enacting resistance to what participants understood as a damaging cultural cycle of hostility and invisibility. Finally, I show that this cultural protest tactic had rich symbolic meaning that went beyond the predictions of social movement research. Insights from this research can (and should) be applied to study tactics that target nonstate actors but tend to fall outside the scope of social movement research.

II. Autoethnography. This is an ethnography of ourselves engaging in a certain kind of activity.

Traversing No Man's Land in Search of An(Other) Identity
Marion Jones, Liverpool John Moores University, Liverpool, United Kingdom.

Abstract

In this autoethnography I provide a reflective-reflexive account of my search for an(other) identity following my move from my native Bavaria to North West England. It is a story of contradiction and uncertainty, which addresses issues of national identity and cultural adaptation. I offer a human portrait of how I experienced the interaction of agency and structure in my endeavor to become British and how I became embroiled in a moral, ethical, and emotional turmoil of conflicting imperatives. The key themes, through which I make explicit the struggle to create a coherent narrative of my self in relation to experiences of belonging, difference, and attachment in social, cultural, and political spaces, are departure and arrival, border crossing, and a disoriented self in transit. In presenting this multilayered account, I employ the technique of performance frames in the form of three literary categories, epic, drama and lyric, through which I revisit critical events and elucidate the gradual process of bringing my innermost feelings and thoughts to the surface. By weaving a rich tapestry of evocative, analytical, and theoretical materials I make explicit the complexities involved in autoethnographic research. Through inviting others to embark with me on this inner journey, I seek to assist those who find themselves similarly suspended in liminal spaces and to engender empathy and understanding among those who act as hosts toward border crossers like myself. Ultimately, I hope that my autoethnography provides a communicative, potentially subversive space, which invites critical reflection and discussion on the intersectionality of collective identities and thereby promotes individuals' freedom to choose, negotiate, and translate their cultural identities freely regardless of their cultural, social, or ethnic origins.

III. Discourse analysis. This is commonly referred to as ideological criticism. It involves identifying and unpacking the ideological forces (the beliefs, assumptions, norms, values, expectations, and fears) that are shaping our understanding of a reality or situation. Discourse analysis has been used to study discourses pertaining to success, patriotism, and war.

A Call to Arms at the End of History: A Discourse–Historical Analysis of George W. Bush's Declaration of War on Terror

Phil Graham, Thomas Keenan & Anne-Maree Dowd, University of Queensland

Abstract

In this article we take a discourse–historical approach to illustrate the significance of George W. Bush's (2001) declaration of a 'war on terror'. We present four exemplary 'call to arms' speeches by Pope Urban II (1095), Queen Elizabeth I (1588), Adolf Hitler (1938) and George W. Bush (2001) to exemplify the structure, function, and historical significance of such texts in western societies over the last millennium. We identify four generic features that have endured in such texts throughout this period: (i) an appeal to a legitimate power source that is external to the orator, and which is presented as inherently good; (ii) an appeal to the historical importance of the culture in which the discourse is situated; (iii) the construction of a thoroughly evil Other; and (iv) an appeal for unification behind the legitimating external power source. We argue further that such texts typically appear in historical contexts characterized by deep crises in political legitimacy.

IV. Textual research involves analyzing all manner of texts to identify themes, patterns, and relationships.

Hazardous Measures: An Interpretive Textual Analysis of Quantitative Sense-making During Crises

Robert Gephart

Abstract

The current paper presents a computer-supported approach to the interpretive analysis of organizational texts and documents. Computer-supported interpretive textual analysis, as presented here, is a qualitative research approach which seeks to provide insights into members' meanings and interpretations. It uses four analytical processes: theoretical sampling, computer software supported text analysis, expansion analysis, and producing textual statistics. Interpretive textual analysis contrasts with quantitative content analysis methods which compose variables from qualitative data and use these variables to test existent theories using inferential statistics. The present paper uses computer supported textual analysis to investigate quantitative sensemaking during a public inquiry into a well blow-out involving hydrogen sulphide gas. I address three research questions relevant to crisis sensemaking. First, what quantitative practices and terms were used in sensemaking about the crisis, and how were these used? Second, how were quantitative practices relevant to the management of risks and hazards? And third, how did sensemaking vary among stakeholder groups, and what were the implications of the variations for organizational action? The results and findings from the computer-supported textual analysis show that quantitative practices and terms played an important role in inquiry sensemaking. The two theoretically meaningful groups involved in the incident used different vocabularies and logics for sensemaking. The government group used a 'step logic' to emphasize formal steps in the management of the hazard. This required the precise measurement of the hazards as a basis for initiating-rule

governed actions to control the hazards. In contrast, the opera-
tor company used a logic of local safeguarding to interpret the
hazards and measurements of the hazards. The paper concludes
by discussing the general methodological and theoretical implica-
tions which interpretive textual analysis has for studies of sense-
making in organizational behavior research.

V. Focus group research. A focus group is a group of people who
are asked about their opinions, perceptions, attitudes, and beliefs
towards a person, service, product, concept, advertisement, idea,
or packaging by a facilitator. The primary attraction of focus group
research is the ability to get immediate findings from a sample population. Focus groups are among the most popularly used qualitative research methods.

Exploring the Knowledge, Attitudes, Beliefs, and Communication
Preferences of the General Public Regarding HPV—Findings
From CDC Focus Group Research and Implications for Practice.
Allison L. Friedman and Hilda Shepeard, Centers for Disease
Control and Prevention, National Center for HIV, STD and TB
Prevention, Division of STD Prevention, Atlanta, Georgia,
Abstract
Genital human papillomavirus (HPV) infection is the most com-
mon sexually transmitted virus in the United States, causing
genital warts, cervical cell abnormalities, and cervical cancer
in women. To inform HPV education efforts, 35 focus groups
were conducted with members of the general public, stratified by
gender, race/ethnicity, and urban/rural location. Focus groups
explored participants' knowledge, attitudes, and beliefs about
HPV and a hypothetical HPV vaccine as well as their commu-
nication preferences for HPV-related educational messages.
Audience awareness and knowledge of HPV were low across all
groups. This, along with an apparent STD-associated stigma,
served as barriers to participants' hypothetical acceptance of a
future vaccine. Although information about HPV's high preva-
lence and link to cervical cancer motivated participants to learn
more about HPV, it also produced audience fear and anxiety. This

research suggests that HPV- and HPV-vaccine-related education efforts must be approached with extreme caution. Other practical implications are discussed.

VI. Conversation analysis. Conversation analysis (CA) is an approach to the study of social interaction, embracing both verbal and non-verbal conduct, in situations of everyday life. It focuses squarely on processes involved in social interaction. CA is commonly referred to as the study of conversations. Its methods and techniques aim to determine the methods and resources that "interactional participants" use and rely on to produce interactional contributions and make sense of the contributions of others.

Toward a Grammar for Dyadic Conversation
Starkey Duncan, Jr., University of Chicago
Abstract

Study of the structure of two-way conversations. Describes signals and rules used by conversants in exchanging turns in conversation. Auditors can either backchannel or make a turn claim signal. Speakers can give turn signals, suppress claims to take a turn by the auditor, or make within-turn signals which mark segments of their (the speaker's) communication. Signals consist of changes in pitch level, loudness, body motions, sequences such as "you know" or "or something" or "drawl" at the end of a turn.

Twenty Seven

Criticisms of Qualitative Research

Although quantitative and qualitative research are of the same epistemological womb, as with most siblings there is bickering and arguing between proponents of the different sides.

> Critics of qualitative research claim that the lack of generalizability is a problem. Indeed, proponents of qualitative research claim that findings are only relevant to the persons under study. The reason being that every population is assumed to be different by being of a different historical, temporal, and cultural context. Qualitative research adheres to this position out of the belief that context is important, and many factors make for a group's context. What we come to know about a group must always be understood in the context that bounds that group.

> Critics of qualitative research contend that qualitative research lacks rigor. Indeed, proponents of qualitative research claim that our fears, values, beliefs, biases, and prejudices shape how we perceive and make sense of things and people. Objectivity is seen as a myth. Qualitative research encourages us to own our biases and prejudices. Qualitative research embraces human subjectivity. Many proponents of qualitative research claim

that trying to control the impact of various forces on human relationships removes the complexity that comes with human affairs. To study the human experience is to grapple with all the complexity and ambiguity that makes us human. Qualitative research promotes the embracing of all this complexity and ambiguity, including all the frustrations that come with doing so.

> Finally, critics of qualitative research contend that qualitative research tends to be self-indulgent and rarely focuses on things that are important. Consequently, qualitative research rarely produces "results" or "findings" that could be used to shape public policy. However, proponents of qualitative research counter that all persons are deserving of study, especially those marginalized. After all, why are certain persons undeserving of study, and how could one claim that certain persons are undeserving of study without ever studying them?

Twenty Eight

Theories, Methodologies & Epistemologies

I n addition to providing the means and devices (methodologies and technologies) that shape how we acquire knowledge, an epistemology also provides the means that shape how we organize and make sense of what that epistemology already defines as knowledge. In the Western/European world we formally use theories (rather than stories) to organize and make sense of our knowledge. In being of the same epistemology, our theories and methodologies are always in harmony with each other. That is, our theories are only capable of describing and organizing the knowledge our methodologies provide, and our methodologies are only capable of proving the knowledge that our theories are capable of organizing. Each legitimizes the other. Our methodologies, technologies, and theories work in tandem to support the status quo. Between our theories and methodologies, no inquiry will ever produce a knowledge that poses a threat to the order of things.

The Western/European world was always destined to be in the theory business. Theories are presumably devoid of human subjectivity. Our biases and prejudices can presumably do nothing to change what the theory of gravity describes. We also like the fact that theories are presumably abstract—devoid of all the flesh and blood that makes us human. The theory of relativity supposedly has no regard for our race, gender, and nationality. We also like the fact that theories are presumably rigorous—testable and verifiable. We can presumably prove whether a theory is true or false. Especially for proponents of quantitative research, this feature is assumed to be valuable for building a reliable knowledge. After all, who can supposedly prove the Native American story that the five Great Lakes were created by God's handprint? Theories play an integral role in our epistemological quest to create a knowledge that exceeds human limitations, meaning a knowledge that is infallible. This is the case against stories. Stories are assumed to be fallible, born out of emotion rather than reason. Stories are also presumably laden with human passion, and thereby inherently unstable and unreliable. Again, who could verify that Moses did split the ocean? Yet the fact is that civilizations that value stories have no interest in proving any story to be true or false. Those are purely our measures born out of our own motives and ambitions. Civilizations that value stories have other means of valuing the worth of a story, such as appreciating a story for its ability to enlarge what we are capable of imagining and becoming.

Nearly every communication curriculum has a required introductory communication theory course. The goal of this course is usually to introduce students to the major theories in communication studies. There will be no mention of any communication stories. These introductory courses will usually begin with defining what is a theory. Students will normally read that a theory is a tool that allows us to predict how the world works. Specifically, a theory is *"a coherent group of tested general propositions, commonly regarded as correct, that can be used as principles of explanation and prediction for a class of phenomena."* Next, students will be introduced to the different ways of assessing the worth of a theory. Foremost, a theory should be logically consistent, be able to offer explanations that are testable, be able to generate new research questions, be able to offer simple explanations, be useful or have practical value, be able to withstand the test of time, and be able to provide broad explanations. Then students will normally read and discuss why theory is important. In Stephen W. Littlejohn's *Theories of Human Communication*, probably the most popular textbook in communication studies, students will read that "The basic justification for studying theories of communication is that they provide a set of useful conceptual tools." Specifically,

> Understanding . . . theories of communication enables the individual to become more competent and adaptive. Teachers often provide students with a list of recipes when beginning the study of communication, but the communication process is too complex to be approached entirely on the level of simplistic guidelines. Students also need to learn about sending and receiving messages and relating to others through an understanding of what happens during communication and an ability to adapt to circumstances. The study of communication theory is a way to obtain this understanding.
>
> Everybody tries to make sense out of their own experience. We assign meaning to what is going on in and around us. Sometimes the meaning is shared and sometimes idiosyncratic. Sometimes it is clear and other times vague or contradictory. Often, however, our interpretation of events reflects sensitivity and clear comprehension. When interpretation is difficult or when confusion results, people often make their theories of interpretation conscious. By developing an understanding of the variety of theories to explain communication, students can interpret communication experiences in more flexible, useful, and discriminating ways. (p. 3)[42]

The rest of these introductory communication courses will usually be devoted to studying the major theories in communication studies.

Syllabus For Communication Theory
COM 305

Required Text: Griffin, E. (1997). A First Look at Communication Theory (3rd edition). McGraw-Hill.

Overview: The Communication discipline has a rich intellectual history stemming from the writings of some of the greatest thinkers in

---

[42] Littlejohn, S. W. (1989). *Theories of communication* (Third Edition). Belmont, CA: Wadsworth.

ancient times and continuing to develop today. How has this happened? How has the discipline taken its shape, and how will it continue to grow in new, ever more promising directions? Part of the answer involves theory building. Theories have been proposed, examined, tested, and either retained or discarded. These theories, in turn, have provided the foundation for new theories which were proposed, examined, tested and retained or discarded...and on it goes. In this course, you will gain a clearer understanding of the Communication discipline as a whole, and you will explore the vibrant relationship between theory building, research, and knowledge. You will examine key theories in detail, considering their relationships with other theories and the insights they provide into human communication. And you will create and examine your own theories about communication behavior; in so-doing, you will become a part of the centuries-old process that has created our current understanding of human interaction.

Semester Schedule

T 8/28   *Course Overview & Introduction*

Th 8/30   *What's a Theory?*

T 9/4   *Defining Communication*

Th 9/6   *Coordinated Management of Meaning Theory*

T 9/11   *Action Assembly Theory*

Th 9/13   *Symbolic Interaction Theory*

T 9/18   *Uncertainty Reduction Theory*

Th 9/20   *Symbolic Convergence Theory*

T 9/25   *Cultivation Theory*

Th 9/27   *Semiotics*

T 10/2   *Constructivism*

Th 10/4   *Attribution Theory*

T 10/9   *Cognitive Dissonance Theory*

Th 10/11   *Dialectical Theory*

T 10/18   *Social Penetration Theory*

T 10/23   *Genderlect & Role Theory*

Th 10/25   *Diffusion Theory*

T 10/30   *Communication Accommodation Theory*

Th 11/1   *Adaptive Structuration Theory*

T 11/6   *Expectancy Violations Theory*

Th 11/8   *Social Judgment Theory*

T 11/13   *Interpersonal Deception Theory*

Th 11/15   *Face Negotiation Theory*

T 11/20   *Communication Privacy Management Theory*

T 11/27   *Social Learning Theory*

Th 11/29   *Agenda-Setting & Spiral of Silence Theories*

T 12/4   Anxiety-Uncertainty Management Theory

Th 12/6   Speech Codes Theory

Major Course Assignments

Application Folder Assignment

I have a couple of goals for this assignment that I think you'll find helpful as you make your way through the course. First, I want to encourage you to apply concepts from Communication Theory to your everyday life. Second, I want you to stop and think for a while each week about the things you're learning. I want you to use the material from this course as a set of Communication Theory colored glasses as you survey the world around you. I want you to monitor what you watch, read, and hear, looking for opportunities to use course concepts in interpreting your surroundings.

For each theory this semester I want you to write a short "application entry" which will be added to a folder and compiled throughout the semester. Each entry should be about a page long (typed, doubled-spaced, normal margins), and it should (a) provide a copy or account of the item/event you have observed/found/identified, then (b) offer your own application of a relevant theory (from the course) to the item/event. In other words, you'll be reading and we'll be talking about a theory (or two) each class day. Your job, then, is to find a way to apply that theory-to put it to work in understanding something from your life.

Theory Chapter Assignment

During the semester, you will have the opportunity to explore a breadth of theories from across the communication discipline. The goal is to help you create a foundation on which you can build understanding of other courses and readings. The unfortunate side-effect of a survey course like this is that you don't really get time to "stop and smell the theories." We move through types of theories and ways of approaching the study and practice of communication so quickly that we don't often linger long enough for you to gain a thorough and in-depth understanding. That's where this assignment (and your future elective course) comes in.

You are to write a book chapter on a theory of your choice, in the same form, of the same substance, and incorporating the same features as the chapters in your text. My plan is to compile these and have them for future students in other courses who come to me asking about the specifics of a given theory. You should read everything written (or at least the most substantive works if there is a plethora of writing on the topic) on your theory, and you should be able to answer any relevant question I or the class can put to you about your theory.

Your assignment, then, is to follow exactly the format in the text, and write a chapter of your own on a theory of your choosing just as though it were going to be included in the next edition [of the required text for this course].

The Western/European hegemony in communication studies means that these introductory communication courses will make no mention of any communication stories. It also means that there will be no discussion in these courses and assigned textbooks of the case against theory. Students will be left with the impression that theory is the only viable and reasonable way to organize and make sense of communication knowledge. There will also be no discussion of the inseparable relation between the theories and the methodologies found in communication curriculums. Students, again, would be left with the impression that theory development is the only viable path to building a reliable communication knowledge. There will also be no discussion that theory development has a civilizational origin, and that understanding such origins is important. Nor will there be any discussion of the epistemological forces and ambitions that brought theory into the world. The making of all these impressions is what colonialism looks like in communication studies.

But there are criticisms of theory that should be included in any discussion of theory and theorizing.

1. *Theorizing gives birth to distant otherness. As ideated generalizations, theories classify observations and theorize people in terms of third-person plural. "They" are the subjects of experiments, and the interviewees of surveys, and the respondents to mail questionnaires. "They" also are the conservatives, the unemployed, the Catholics, and the terrorists. All of "them" are neatly labeled and assigned to particular classes on account of characteristics that all members of such classes are assumed to share. Classification already begins at the data-gathering stage of social research . . .*

    In everyday languaging, third-person pronouns refer to those absent. Theorizing makes this absence a seeming virtue that gives theorists the freedom to characterize others in ways radically different and inferior to themselves. Whether one calls this a professional disability (a deafness to individual voices or an institutionalized disrespect for otherness), theorizing is responsible for estranging others from us. (pp. 8-9)

2. *Theorizing trivializes others by reducing them to obedient mechanisms. As spectators, social scientists observe human behaviors, including verbal interactions, from outside the spectacle. From this perspective, behaviors appear as linear sequences, temporally ordered chains of events, or trajectories in a Cartesian space within predefined coordinates. To understand the trajectories, natural scientists would seek to discover their regularities. However, the very mention of "regularities" assumes that trajectories are followed without much choice in the matter. And talk of their "discovery" tends to suggest that they existed prior to their observations and measurement. (p. 9)*

3. *Theorizing creates the very unsocial conditions in which theories can survive, if only by inscribing its monologism into*

observational data. At moments of contact between theorist and theorized, social research greatly depends of collaboration and dialogue...Yet, after signing the consent form, their ability to understand the nature of their involvement and to say "no" to practices they might consider unconscionable is rarely ever called upon again, does not enter the data, and has therefore little chance to inform a theory that speaks to these subjects' capabilities. To uphold the notion that theory is responsive to observations only, the dialogical nature of the actual contact must be hidden; the very collaboration needed to conclude an experiment, concealed. (p. 10)[43]

An introductory communication theory course that recognizes these kinds of criticisms of theory would have syllabus space for stories. In this space students will be introduced to the various components in stories and why so many civilizations view stories as a viable way of situating and organizing knowledge. Students will also be introduced to the distinct attributes of stories, come to recognize the different ways of valuing and appreciating stories, and probe why so many of the world's great knowledges remain woven in stories.

---

[43] Krippendorff, K. (2000). *On the Otherness that Theory Creates*. http://repository. upenn.edu/cgi/viewcontent.cgi?article=1310&context=asc_papers

Twenty Nine

Pedagogy & Epistemology

B esides supplying our theories, methodologies, and technologies, our epistemologies also supply our pedagogies. In other words, in shaping how we define, organize, and acquire knowledge, our epistemologies also shape how we share and promote knowledge. Naturally, how we share our knowledge will be in harmony with how we define, acquire, and organize knowledge. This reality is most evident in communication studies.

How we approach the teaching and learning of communication perpetuates our popular definition of communication. We view teaching as instruction that is fundamentally about imparting information about communication. We strive to find the most effective and efficient ways of sharing, imparting, and distributing our information about communication. We are the *senders* of this information. We aspire to send this information without noise and confusion. Our students are presumably the receivers of this information about communication. We strive to have our students fully absorb all of this information. We stress regurgitation in order to achieve the full reception of our information about communication. We also use tests and assignments to measure what exactly our students are receiving, learning, and knowing. Learning is presumably about reception—our ability to fully absorb the information that is being given to us. Thus learning outcomes are necessary and are always explicitly stated on our syllabuses. But, most importantly, learning outcomes and objectives must always be quantifiable, measurable, and observable. We must be able to objectively demonstrate that learning objectives are being met. The class must be a success.

Align Assessments with Objectives

Assessments should provide us, the instructors, and the students with evidence of how well the students have learned what we intend them to learn. What we want students to learn and be able to do should guide the choice and design of the assessment. There are two major reasons for aligning assessments with learning objectives. First, alignment increases the probability that we will provide students with the opportunities to learn and practice the knowledge and skills that will be required on the various assessments we design. Second, when assessments and objectives are aligned, "good grades" are more likely to translate into "good learning". When objectives and assessments are misaligned, many students will focus their efforts on activities that will lead to good grades on assessments, rather than focusing their efforts on learning what we believe is important.

There are many different types of activities that can be used to assess students' proficiency on a given learning objective, and the same activity can be used to assess different objectives. To ensure more accurate assessment of student proficiencies, it is recommended that you use different kinds of activities so that students have multiple ways to practice and demonstrate their knowledge and skills.

When deciding on what kind of assessment activities to use, it is helpful to keep in mind the following questions:

- *What will the student's work on the activity (multiple choice answers, essays, project, presentation, etc) tell me about their level of competence on the targeted learning objectives?*
- *How will my assessment of their work help guide students' practice and improve the quality of their work?*

- *How will the assessment outcomes for the class guide my teaching practice?*[44]

The modern school system is obsessed with assessing and measuring learning outcomes. Teaching must produce measurable, quantifiable, and observable results. We need to know what exactly our students are learning. What techniques help teachers impart information effectively and efficiently? What makes for high levels of absorption? How and what kinds of technology enable the sharing and imparting of information? In the end, the student is assumed to be an object of instruction, an object of communication. What passes for classroom communication is merely about facilitating learning outcomes and objectives. The learning outcomes have already be set and determined. All that remains is to figure out how these outcomes and objectives will be reliably achieved and measured.

There is no communication in the communication classroom. There is no negotiation or deliberation over learning outcomes and objectives. There is no communication about learning, no exploration or consideration of different definitions of learning and teaching. There is no invitation to look anew at what communication means and the relation between communication and what being human means. Nor is there any invitation to look at the cultural and civilizational origins of our popular definitions of communication. The notion of communication being a transactional process is assumed to be universally true. The lack of any communication in the communication classroom means that the communication classroom impedes the moral imagination of our students. Without any opportunity to fundamentally disrupt anything, our students can only obey and submit.

The communication classroom, in operating on popular transactional notions of communication, promotes submission and subordination. Power remains with the person teaching, the person sending and imparting the information, the person determining the learning outcomes. All that remains is for the student to learn—to absorb what is being instructed and transmitted. In this way, the communication

---

[44] *The Whys and Hows of Assessment.* Carnegie Mellon University. http://www.cmu.edu/teaching/assessment/howto/basics/objectives.html

classroom aids and abets an ideology of submission. It prepares students for a life of submission and subordination. There will be no communication in this life, or at least none that could present new meanings and understandings that possibly threaten the status quo. There will only be instruction, regurgitation, and submission. The communication classroom works in harmony with other institutions to keep us obedient by discouraging communication. We will never become a threat to the status quo as our popular models of communication undercut our being able to imagine the world anew. So as much as the communication classroom promises to be promoting education by effectively delivering information about communication, this is nothing but an illusion. Our popular definitions of communication make education impossible by cultivating only submission and subordination. In order for education to be possible, new definitions of communication must arise that promote and encourage the exploration and formation of new meanings and understandings. Communication, education, and liberation are bound up with each other. To communicate is to educate, and to educate is to emancipate, to arrive at a new meaning or understanding of something that fundamentally enlarges our sense of what is possible.

A Case Study
Inventing Effective Teaching & Learning

Separation is the foundation of the western/European worldview. Separation means that one thing is outside of and different from another thing. We find this separation between good and evil, heaven and hell, male and female, order and chaos, knowledge and ignorance, teaching and learning, mind and body, light and darkness, health and disease, and so forth. In communication theory this separation makes for meaning and ambiguity, communication and confusion, verbal and nonverbal communication, speech and silence, encoders and decoders, message and medium, speakers and listeners. Our communication theories, pedagogies, and methodologies begin with definitions of communication that assume separation, and consequently help concretize the idea that separation is real. This reality can be seen in a paper titled

"College Student Learning, Motivation, and Satisfaction as a Function of Effective Instructor Communication Behaviors" in the *Southern Communication Journal* (March 2014). Drawing upon an extensive body of communication literatures, the paper highlights various findings about teaching:

> *Instructors arrive at the classroom with two simultaneous goals: rhetorical goals and relational goals. Instructors who teach to meet rhetorical goals focus primarily on using classroom communication as a way to influence or persuade their students so that student learning and understanding occurs. This goal is instructor centered in that instructors act primarily as sources of information and students act as passive receivers of information, with an emphasis placed on message design that facilitates effective instruction.*

> *Conversely, instructors who teach to meet relational goals focus primarily on engaging in classroom communication to develop a professional working relationship with their students. This goal is student centered in that instructors and students communicate together collaboratively with an emphasis placed on the role of shared emotions and feelings that enable both students and instructors to interact both effectively and affectively with each other. Effective teaching requires instructors to meet both their rhetorical goals and their relational goals. To communicate effectively with students (i.e., teach to meet rhetorical goals), instructors must engage in clarity and should integrate humor into their teaching. Clarity, which is considered to be the extent to which instructors effectively employ verbal and nonverbal messages to communicate knowledge in a way that facilitates student understanding, contains a content dimension and a structural dimension. Content clarity is demonstrated by speaking fluently and avoiding the use of vague or ambiguous statements and examples, whereas structural clarity is demonstrated by organizing the presentation of material such as using previews, transitions, and summaries. Humor, which is considered to be intentional verbal and nonverbal communication aimed towards achieving a desired response in a receiver, typically in the form of laughter or other indicators of spontaneous*

pleasure or delight, can range from the use of puns, jokes, and anec-dotes to self- and student-disparagement and is used by instructors as a way to clarify course content for their students.

To communicate affectively with students (i.e., teach to meet rela-tional goals), instructors should engage in immediacy behaviors, communicate in a confirming manner and express caring toward their students. Immediacy consists of behaviors that reduce physical and psychological distance between students and instructors through instructor use of nonverbal behaviors such as eye contact, smil-ing, use of gestures, and vocal variety and verbal behaviors such as addressing students by name, asking students questions, and praising student work. Confirmation occurs when instructors communicate to their students that they are worthwhile and significant individu-als by responding to students' questions and comments, demonstrat-ing an interest in their students, and teaching in an interactive style. Caring signifies to students that their instructors are concerned with their welfare by communicating in a manner that is understanding, empathic, and responsive.

Affective learning involves student feelings, emotions, and degrees of acceptance toward the subject matter, whereas cognitive learning ranges from the simple retention of information to complex synthesis of material. Positive relationships exist between perceived instructor clarity, humor, immediacy, confirmation, and caring and both stu-dent reports of their affective learning and cognitive learning. At the same time, however, researchers have found that positive relation-ships exist among several of these behaviors. For example, instruc-tors who are immediate are considered to be clear, confirming, caring, and humorous and instructors who are humorous are considered to be caring.

When students perceive their instructors as using a variety of rhetori-cal and relational teaching behaviors simultaneously, their learning outcomes can be enhanced. When instructors were considered to be confirming and caring, students were likely to be higher in course and instructor affect, cognitive learning indicators, and communication satisfaction. Research suggests that students perceive these types of teaching behavior as a motivator in the classroom as students appreciate instructors who listen to class comments and want to be involved with them, in part because when instructors respond to student questions, solicit participation and take student opinion into consideration, they are communicating to students that their input is valued. As such, instructors who are perceived as responding to student questions, demonstrating an interest in their students, and utilizing an interactive teaching style (all components of instructor confirmation) as well as caring share one common element: They recognize that students are an essential component of the instructional process. By being both task and relationally oriented in their teaching, confirming and caring instructors implicitly inform their students that they are interested in their students' academic success.

This paper assumes a separation between teaching (teachers) and learning (learners). The goal of the paper is to identify what communication practices work in promoting learning and thereby make for effective instruction. We are to assume that "effective teaching" is measurable and quantifiable. We can presumably reliably identify who is an effective teacher and what makes for effective teaching.

But no amount of clarity and humor can affect what a person is ready and willing to learn. Learning begins and ends with what a person is ready and willing to understand. This paper also assumes that learning is about acquiring knowledge of things. It happens in our grasping of the material that is determined to be important. Learning becomes a subservient process. Teachers determine what students learn. School administrators, in shaping and enforcing our courses and curriculums, also determine what students learn. Ultimately, learning as acquiring knowledge makes for subordination, minds that are dependent on other minds for direction and instruction.

In reality learning is about being born anew. It is about coming to a new way of understanding and experiencing the world. Learning emerges in the expansion of our moral, emotional, spiritual, and mental selves. No doubt, teachers can encourage and even seduce us to look at the world anew, but to be willing to do so is all on us. Learning involves courage, persistence, and perseverance.

Separation reduces teaching to a set of communication skills and techniques. Teaching becomes a process of equipping students with a set of skills and knowledge, and the goal is to do so effectively. However, assuming the role and responsibility for what students learn involves enlarging our egos and our sense of importance. It means believing that one person has the power to shape the minds of others. It also means believing that one person has the right to determine and dictate what another should learn.

But what of the separation that is found in communication theory? We are to assume that the mind of the encoder is outside and separate from the mind of the decoder. Communication is presumably about these different minds sharing, exchanging, and transacting different kinds of messages. That is, communication is assumed to be an expression of mind, as in our assumption that eloquence and coherence reflect a superior mind. We assume that mind and communication are separate and outside from each other. But because communication is assumed to be an expressive rather than constitutive of mind, the study of communication becomes secondary to the study of mind. Moreover, although we value communication and the study of communication, as in helping us enhance teaching and learning, the teaching and studying never rises to how communication constitutes of our minds, and in so doing, creates our worlds.

The popular view is that mind comes from biology, and that the capacity of our minds can be reliably measured. We continue to believe that our most important accomplishments will come from persons with supposedly great minds and that our prosperity requires the cultivation of these minds. We therefore also tend to believe that communication has no significant capacity to truly achieve anything great, nor can it significantly contribute to our progress and prosperity.

All of these beliefs can be found in immigration debates where the focus continues to be on attracting "the right kinds of people" and discouraging "the wrong kind of people." In the end, communication studies remains bereft of any compelling discussion of ethics and knowledge. At best, communication studies promises to contribute to how communication can improve our doing of different things, such as teaching and learning. But we can demonstrate that the separation that we assume in communication theory is without foundation. Meaning is never outside of ambiguity. In being laden with ambiguity, every utterance, every gesture, lends for multiple meanings. Speech and silence also bound up with each other. Speech silences speech, just as much as silence silences speech. But, most importantly, the separation between mind and communication is without foundation, nothing but an illusion. Communication is a product of mind, just as mind is a product of communication. We can demonstrate this in different ways.

I. *Solitary Confinement*

    a. If our minds are truly independent of other minds, and thus supposedly have no need for other minds, why then does solitary confinement destroy our minds?

II. *Language Trends Matter*

    Because language plays an integral role in the shaping of our minds, language trends—as in how a society uses language and to what ends—play an important role in shaping our minds.

III. *Language Shapes Policy That Affects Us All*

    We use language to create, shape, and influence public policy. Public policy affects how resources and privileges will be allocated—that is, public policy determines who gets what resources and privileges. Consequently, those whose language is shaping public policy often stand to benefit most from public policy.

IV. *The Power Of The Communication Of Others To Affect Us*

    How other human beings nurture us and communicate with us as children has a profound impact on the shaping of our minds.

V. Language, Communication, and Intersubjectivity

The language we use to create our minds is always given to us. Besides symbols and rules, every language also comes with a worldview that influences how we perceive and experience the world. To share a language is to share a worldview. In other words, when minds share a language, they also share a worldview. Thus no mind that uses a common language can be truly independent of other minds.

That mind is bound up with communication means that mind is malleable. It can change and evolve. It also means—or reminds us—that mind is bound up with the body, and with the world. Mind is bound up with the body because meaning is bound up with ambiguity. Thus, no meaning is stable and complete. Ambiguity keeps meaning in motion. We never know for certain what things mean. We estimate and approximate, often relying on our instincts and impulses. The ambiguity that permeates meaning guarantees that meaning will never submit perfectly to us. We will always have to grapple with meaning, which means that even our best descriptions will be laden with ambiguity. Mind is also bound up with body, and the body must physically deal with the limits of time and space. Time and space, or history and geography, play an integral role in shaping our meanings and relations to ambiguity. No mind can escape the limits of time and space. Such limits speak to our fallibility and mortality, reminding us of the presence of the body in all things.

But the dominant epistemology in the western/European world remains determined to remove the body from our descriptions of things. Presumably, the body makes for subjectivity by being laden with passions and emotions, biases and prejudices, instincts and impulses. It must therefore be always ruled, disciplined, and controlled. We aspire to produce descriptions that defy the limits of time and space. We also aspire to achieve descriptions that reflect neither our fallibility nor mortality, which means that every attempt must be made to remove all that the body acknowledges, such as the reality of history and geography. Such is what the making of the delusion of separation looks like.

To acknowledge that mind is always bound up with the body is to recognize the need to be always probing and excavating. Even the notion of mind and body warrants scrutiny. Case in point, the authors of the paper, "College Student Learning, Motivation, and Satisfaction as a Function of Effective Instructor Communication Behaviors", are aiming to use quantitative methods to produce a truth about teaching and learning that is outside of time and space. There is no acknowledgement of the body, that is, no discussion of history (culture) and geography. We are simply to assume that teaching is universally about imparting knowledge, and doing so effectively. We are also to assume that teaching universally involves a common set of processes. In other words, there is no recognition of even the possibility of different definitions and interpretations of effective teaching and learning. The authors of this paper would have us believe that the study that forms the foundation of the paper has nothing do with ideology. It is just science. We are to believe that the authors' values, beliefs, fears, ambitions, and experiences have nothing to do with how the study was framed and conducted. We are also to assume that the goal and findings of the study serve no ideological mission and function. Presumably, all peoples benefit equally from viewing teaching and learning the way the authors do. But, again, such is what the authors would have us assume. The separation is unrelenting. From the mind/body separation (or delusion) comes the separation (or delusion) between science and politics.

The notions of effective teaching and learning are nothing but social constructs. We brought these things into the world, and did so for a variety of reasons. These came into the world by how we already perceive the world. That is, to believe that human potentiality is measurable and quantifiable lends naturally for believing that teaching and learning are measurable and quantifiable. Also, believing that teaching and learning are measurable and quantifiable would have us believe that we have the ability to remove the mystery from these processes. We now (presumably) have control over these processes. This gaining of control over human processes helps fulfill our mission of trying to gain control over the world. Effectively doing so means removing the ambiguity and uncertainty from teaching and learning. It means us being in control of those processes. It means that the outcomes are now predictable and controllable. It means, most of all, that our mission to control all of the world is possible and realizable. All of this, again, is supposedly evident in the fact that the students in the study are reporting improved learning outcomes as a result of the instructor employing various rhetorical and relational practices.

But what exactly are the students learning? Are the students learning anything important? We are told that the students report improved learning outcomes. But how did this become the measure of improved learning? Or, why and how did the measure of improved learning become something that is measurable and quantifiable? Moreover, how did all learning become measurable and quantifiable? Indeed, rather than focusing on learning, the paper focuses on learning outcomes, specifically on how to improve learning outcomes. We are to assume that improved learning outcomes constitute learning, and that learning is evidenced by improved learning outcomes. Likewise, effective teaching becomes or is measured by our ability to increase learning outcomes. An effective teacher presumably improves learning outcomes. From this standpoint, no prophet was an effective teacher. Indeed, what was any prophet teaching that was measurable and quantifiable? What also were we to learn that was measurable and quantifiable? In fact, which prophet taught anything that was so?

Oscar Wilde said that nothing that is worth learning can be taught. Indeed, learning begins with us. We determine what we learn by what we are willing to believe and imagine. Learning involves every dimension of our being, mind, body, and spirit. This again is why learning—or the learning of anything profound—is so hard and often impossible. Yet learning should be hard. That it should be so means that learning should involve every dimension of our being. Only by involving every dimension of our being can learning make for a fundamentally new way of understanding ourselves and the world. That is, only by being hard does learning become valuable.

Thirty

Constructing Hegemony in Communication Studies

The Association

A worldview achieves hegemony by controlling and commanding nearly all the practices, structures, and institutions that impact how we perceive and make sense of things. This kind of hegemony can be found in communication studies. In communication research textbooks there is no mention of the many methodologies found in oral based civilizations. We are to assume that the list of quantitative and qualitative research methods captures all the methods that are available to us to study communication. We are also to assume that African, Asian, Middle Eastern, and Native American civilizations have no methods that are valuable enough to be deserving of inclusion in communication textbooks and curriculums. Nor are there communication job descriptions for persons with expertise in methods that fall outside the quantitative/qualitative research axis. All these kinds of absences and erasures reflect colonialism.

The epistemology that is of the dominant worldview in communication studies assumes that communication is inherently a linguistic and symbolic process. Thus communication is presumably observable, quantifiable, and measureable. The dominant worldview in communication studies promotes this view of communication by controlling nearly all the practices, structures, and institutions that bear on the teaching and studying of communication. This hegemony can be seen in the mission of the national association that governs most communication departments, the scholarly journals that control the dissemination of communication research, the job descriptions for openings in communication departments, the selection of the editors and referees who will control what papers will be published in communication journals and the kinds of scholarly books that will be published, and the kinds of courses that constitute communication curriculums. Simply put, this hegemony is profound. What emerges from this hegemony is the perpetuation of a knowledge of communication that is in harmony with a Western/European worldview, and consequently will never pose a threat to anything.

National Communication Association (NCA)

NCA is a scholarly society and as such works to enhance the research, teaching, and service produced by its members on topics of both intellectual and social significance. Staff at the NCA National Office follow trends in national research, teaching, and service priorities. It both relays those opportunities to its members and represents the academic discipline of communication in those national efforts.

NCA is the oldest and largest national organization to promote communication scholarship and education. Founded in 1914 as the National Association of Academic Teachers of Public Speaking, the society incorporated in 1950 as the Speech Association of America. The organization changed its name to Speech Communication Association, in 1970. It adopted its present name in 1997.

NCA takes the lead in publicizing the discipline's scholarship through press releases and regular contacts with policy makers. When appropriate, NCA offers scholarship to support the development of governmental policy. Where proposed laws are of interest or potential concern, the NCA National Office staff notifies members so that they can make their opinions known to their representatives on Capitol Hill.

NCA sponsors an annual convention, which is the leading outlet for the discipline's scholarship. NCA's summer conferences bring together scholars working in an emerging area of interest to exchange ideas. NCA publishes nine academic journals, which are the leading publications in their area of specialty.

In sum, NCA is the institutional arm of communication studies. It maintains institutional order by controlling the administration of communication studies in the United States and around the world, as in owning and controlling many of the most prestigious journals that shape our knowledge of communication, as well as hosting and organizing the largest annual conference of communication teachers, scholars, and students from the United States and around the world.

Thirty One

Constructing Hegemony in Communication Studies

The Journals

Besides controlling the mission of the national association that governs most communication departments, the hegemony of the Western/European worldview in communication studies also commands the scholarly journals that control the dissemination of communication research, and thereby control what kind of scholarship is seen as legitimate and worthy of consideration for rewards and inclusion in tenure and promotion portfolios.

Human Communication Research
Human Communication Research publishes the best empirical research examining communication processes and effects. Major topic areas for the journal include language and social interaction, nonverbal communication, interpersonal communication, organizational communication and new technologies, group communication, mass communication, health communication, intergroup/intercultural communication, and developmental issues in communication, but research examining other areas relevant to the study of communication is welcome.

Successful submissions to the journal will (a) test or develop theory in the field of communication, (b) be methodologically rigorous, (c) be clearly and concisely written, and (d) address the connections between the research and broader concerns within society. Quantitative research should include clear descriptions of measurement reliability and validity, measures of effect size for all significant effects, measures of variability to accompany all measures of central tendency, and power estimates when results are non-significant. Discussion of results should attend to effect size as well as statistical significance. Qualitative work should discuss procedures employed to assure the validity of interpretations (e.g., negative case analysis, member-checking), as well as provide detailed presentations of data that demonstrate the empirical basis for claims. All research should provide descriptions of data collection and analysis procedures that are accurate, lucid, and comprehensive.

Communication Reports

Communication Reports (CR) publishes original manuscripts that are short, data/text-based, and related to the broadly defined field of human communication. The mission of the journal is to showcase exemplary scholarship without censorship based on topics, methods, or analytical tools. Articles that are purely speculative or theoretical, and not data analytic, are not appropriate for this journal. Authors are expected to devote a substantial portion of the manuscript to analyzing and reporting research data. Research articles should be 5000 words or less. This restriction includes the abstract, text of the document, references, footnotes, appendices, and the captions for tables and figures, but slightly longer manuscripts may be considered.

Journal of Communication
The Journal of Communication is a general forum for communication scholarship and publishes articles and book reviews examining a broad range of issues in communication theory and research. JoC publishes

the best available scholarship on all aspects of communication. All methods of scholarly inquiry into communication are welcome. Manuscripts should be conceptually meaningful, methodologically sound, interesting, clearly written, and thoughtfully argued.

Ordinarily (unless a compelling argument is made), data- or text-based manuscripts must follow specific guidelines depending upon method. Quantitative manuscripts should report reliability estimates for dependent variables, the amount of variance accounted for in significance tests, and power when a result is not significant. When measures of central tendency are reported, appropriate measures of variability should be included. Quantitative content analyses should report inter-coder reliability, preferably using a statistic that controls for agreement by chance. Survey research should describe the population, sampling procedures, and response rate. Qualitative research should articulate the standards employed to assure the quality and verification of the interpretation presented (e.g., member-checking, negative case analysis).

Communication Monographs

Communication Monographs, published in March, June, September & December, reports original, theoretically grounded research dealing with human symbolic exchange across the broad spectrum of interpersonal, group, organizational, cultural and mediated contexts in which such activities occur. The scholarship reflects diverse modes of inquiry and methodologies that bear on the ways in which communication is shaped and functions in human interaction.

The journal endeavours to publish the highest quality communication social science manuscripts that are grounded theoretically. The manuscripts aim to expand, qualify or integrate existing theory or additionally advance new theory. The journal is not restricted to particular theoretical or methodological perspectives. Manuscripts reflecting diverse issues, scholarly modes of inquiry, and innovative thinking about the ways in which communication is shaped and functions in human interaction are presented.

Unless specifically indicated otherwise, articles in this journal have undergone rigorous peer review, including screening by the editor and review by at least two anonymous referees.

Thirty Two

Constructing Hegemony in Communication Studies

The Jobs & Careers

B esides controlling the mission of the national association that governs most communication departments, commanding the scholarly journals that control the dissemination of communication research, and thereby controlling what kind of scholarship is seen as legitimate and worthy of consideration for rewards and inclusion in tenure and promotion portfolios, the hegemony of the Western/ European worldview in communication studies also controls the job descriptions and thereby who will get to teach in communication departments, who will get the resources to study communication and write scholarly articles and books about communication, who will develop the courses and curriculums, and, probably most importantly, who will get to guide and shape the development of the next generation of communication teachers and researchers. Naturally, most of these job ads will be for persons who view communication as a linguistic and symbolic process, and especially for persons with expertise in quantitative research.

Penn State University
Department of Communication Arts and Sciences

*The Department of Communication Arts and Sciences at The
Pennsylvania State University seeks a tenure-track assistant or associate professor whose research and teaching are in interpersonal or
family communication, broadly construed. We are particularly interested in those candidates who have a demonstrated interest in empirical theory building with expertise in quantitative methods.*

*Candidates should provide clear evidence of scholarly and teaching
excellence. In addition to conducting research and teaching undergraduate and graduate courses, duties include course development
in the area of specialty, supervision of theses and dissertations, and
involvement in other departmental activities. Additional consider-
ations in reviewing candidates include experience with grant-based
research, interest in trans-disciplinary research, and an appreciation
of working alongside diverse colleagues in both the social sciences and
humanities.*

*We encourage applications from individuals of diverse backgrounds.
Employment will require successful completion of background
check(s) in accordance with University policies. Penn State is committed to affirmative action, equal opportunity, and diversity of its
workplace.*

*The Department of Communication at Michigan State University
seeks an individual for a tenure-track faculty position in computer-
mediated communication/social media with an emphasis on interpersonal effects in a variety of relationships and/or professional settings
such as personal relationships, internal and/or external organizational relationships, online education, doctor/patient interactions,
environmental and risk communication, community-building, and
online social support.*

*Qualified applicants will have a social scientific focus and emphasize
communication theory, expertise in quantitative research methods,
and ability to teach both graduate and undergraduate courses. We
seek candidates with a strong track record or potential for a visible
research agenda who will mentor students and contribute to the
department's strong doctoral program. The successful candidate will*

teach and expand current course offerings in computer-mediated communication, interpersonal communication, research methods, and/ or organizational communication. Applicants who pursue funded scholarly research opportunities in the study of CMC are especially encouraged to apply. A PhD in Communication, Social Psychology, Information Science, or a related social science discipline is required. Major responsibilities will include an active and productive publication agenda, teaching two courses per semester, and pursuit of a funded research program through active grant writing.

MSU is an equal opportunity/affirmative action institution. MSU is committed to achieving excellence through cultural diversity. The university actively encourages applications and/or nominations of women, persons of color, veterans and persons with disabilities.

The Department of Communication at Portland State University (PSU) seeks a full-time, nine-month, tenure-track, Assistant Professor. The department seeks a scholar who is well grounded in fundamental theories of (mass) media communication and who has specific expertise in new/social media and/or mobile communication. The ideal candidate will also have expertise: (1) that complements existing departmental strengths in interpersonal, health, political, cognitive, or cultural communication; and (2) in teaching introductory quantitative research methods at both the undergraduate and graduate level. Job requirements include publishing research, effectively teaching undergraduate and graduate students, participating in departmental and university service, and pursuing external funding. PSU is the largest university in the Oregon University System, with approximately 29,000 students. PSU is an Affirmative-Action, Equal-Opportunity Institution and welcomes applications from candidates who support diversity. Women and members of minority groups are encouraged to apply. Review of applications will begin Friday, November 1st, and will continue until the position is filled.

Boston University's College of Communication invites candidates to apply for 2 Assistant Professor tenure-track positions in Emerging

Media Studies. These positions will be part of an exciting new program at the College that addresses the study of emerging media in the context of the College's already strong programs in traditional media research. This includes the development of new M.A. and Ph.D. programs and a cross-unit Center for Mobile Communication Studies. These positions require a Ph.D. in Communication or related area at the time of hire, with strong grounding in theory and research, teaching experience and a publication record. Candidates with potential to establish a funded research program are especially encouraged to apply.

Areas of particular interest to the search committee include the following, ideally in combination:

(1) Mobile communication studies. Methodological sophistication in quantitative analysis of longitudinal behavioral data concerning political or interpersonal communication would be especially desirable.

(2) Big data. Quantitative analysis of human communication behavior related to emerging media technology. Skills in topics such as data mining, secondary analysis of large data sets, visual displays of quantitative information, and dynamic data mapping are of particular interest. The candidates should have previously connected these skills with substantive topics related to emerging media studies or journalism.

(3) Creative behaviors of social media users. Rigorous social scientific analysis of user behavior related to co-creation and consumption of emerging media content. Of particular interest is the relationship between these activities and traditional media and social media entrepreneurship.

The University of Michigan Department of Communication Studies seeks applicants for a tenure track/tenured position. We seek a quantitative social scientist to complement and extend current faculty interests and strengths in media effects, political communication and/ or media psychology. The department seeks a scholar who studies the societal and individual effects of traditional and/or emerging media and whose methods include experiments, surveys, longitudinal studies, content analysis, meta analysis, "big data" analytics, network analysis, or other quantitative social science techniques. While all areas of emphasis will be considered, we are particularly interested in applicants whose work focuses on political communication and/or media psychology, and who are able to contribute meaningfully to the teaching and mentoring mission of the department.

The University of Michigan is an equal opportunity/affirmative action employer. Women and minorities are encouraged to apply.

The Department of Communication Studies at the University of Georgia seeks to fill a tenure-track faculty position of Interpersonal Communication with secondary interest in Health Communication at the rank of Assistant Professor, beginning August 2013. The successful candidate will teach large lecture undergraduate courses in interpersonal communication, quantitative research methods and/ or health communication, as well as courses in communication theory, advanced interpersonal communication, and topics related to his or her research interests. At the graduate level, successful candidates will teach seminars in communication theory, quantitative research methods, health communication, and topics related to his or her research. A Ph.D. in Communication is required by the time of appointment. Potential to seek external funding is desired. Salary is commensurate with experience.

The Franklin College of Arts and Sciences, its many units, and the University of Georgia are committed to increasing the diversity of its faculty and students, and sustaining a work and learning environment that is inclusive. Women, minorities and people with disabilities are strongly encouraged to apply. The University is an EEO/AA institution.

The Department of Communication at the University of Missouri - St. Louis (UMSL) invites applications for a tenure-track Assistant Professor or a tenured Associate Professor. An earned PhD in

Communication or an equivalent degree is required for consideration as an Associate Professor with tenure. A PhD in hand is preferred at the Assistant Professor rank as well, although ABD candidates will be given full consideration.

The Department of Communication is one of the largest and most productive departments on campus with a strong culture of independent and collaborative quantitative research.
The ideal candidate will have (1) the ability to teach quantitative research methods at the graduate and/or undergraduate level; (2) a background in online education; and (3) a demonstrated familiarity with new communication technologies. In addition to these qualifications, expertise in one of the following specializations is also desirable: (a) CMC/Social Media/New Media; (b) Health Communication; (c) Interpersonal/Organizational Communication; or (d) Mass Communication.

The School of Communication at The Ohio State University invites applicants for an open rank position in the area of political communication with an emphasis on mass communication, interpersonal communication, communication technology, or some combination of the three.
The School is committed to empirical, social-scientific research on communication processes, either basic or applied, making original and substantively important contributions, and is regularly ranked among the top communication research programs in the country. We seek colleagues who will help us continue this tradition and can envision research projects and courses that will be attractive to graduate and undergraduate students from within the major, and speak to the interests and needs of non-majors. We have recently renovated a number of research labs and teaching facilities to support quality research and teaching. All of our positions involve research, teaching, and a service component.
Qualifications: Candidates must have a Ph.D. degree in communication or related social science field or be ABD . . . . Applicants should

have a demonstrated record or strong likelihood of publication in top-tier journals as well as evidence of effective teaching. Applicants for tenured positions must have both a strong publication record reflecting theoretically-driven interests and an international reputation for high-quality research. A record of external funding is also highly desirable for applicants for tenured positions. Interests in international communication or urban studies are attractive but not essential.

To build a diverse workforce Ohio State encourages applications from individuals with disabilities, minorities, veterans, and women. EEO/AA employer.

The Department of Communication Studies at the University of Georgia seeks to fill a faculty position in Health Communication at the rank of Associate or Full Professor with tenure. The candidate will teach health communication as well as other courses within her or his research areas. Minimum requirements are a Ph.D. in Communication or a related field as well as a strong record of published and externally funded research. Expertise in quantitative methods is desired. Salary and start up funds are commensurate with experience.

The department has a competitive and nationally ranked M.A. and Ph.D. program and an active research faculty with a consistent record of extramural funding, scholarly publication, and teaching excellence. The Franklin College of Arts and Sciences, its many units, and the University of Georgia are committed to increasing the diversity of its faculty and students, and sustaining a work and learning environment that is inclusive. Women, minorities and people with disabilities are strongly encouraged to apply. The University is an EEO/AA institution.

The Department of Communication Sciences at the University of Connecticut has reopened the search in the area of health communication. Applications will now be accepted for a tenured or tenure-track professor at the Advanced Assistant, Associate, or Full Professor level. Minimum qualifications: Candidates must have university teaching experience, administrative experience, evidence of research productivity and publications, and a completed PhD in Communication or related field. The successful candidate must have the ability to conduct research, teach both undergraduate and graduate courses, and perform professional service commensurate with rank. Applicants must also have the ability to teach quantitative research methods, health communication, and other courses such as advertising, public relations, social networks, new communication technologies, social marketing/communication campaigns, dissemination/translation, or the study, design, and development of media and social networks for health applications. Applicants must have the ability to work in a collegial manner with a diverse faculty, staff and student population. It is preferred candidates possess the ability to contribute through research, teaching, and /or public engagement to the diversity and excellence of the learning experience, as well as the ability to obtain external grant funding to support their research is desirable.

The University is ranked among US News and World Report's top 20 public institutions. The Communication Program is ranked Number 1 in New England according to the National Research Council and ranks among the six most research-productive nationally. The program serves approximately 450 undergraduate majors, 10 M.A. and 35 Ph.D. students. The University of Connecticut encourages minorities, women, and people with disabilities to apply for this position.

The Department of Communication Arts at the University of Wisconsin-Madison seeks a social scientist for a tenured or tenure-track faculty position in Communication Science to begin Fall. Candidates with a Ph. D. in Communication or an affiliated social science discipline will be considered. A successful candidate must demonstrate strong quantitative methodological competency and conduct research via social scientific methods in any of the areas pertinent to interpersonal communication and social influences, including (but not limited to) interpersonal relationships, family communication, interpersonal influence, message production, persuasion, nonverbal communication, and social networks. Candidates should be able to teach courses at the undergraduate and graduate levels, and develop and/or maintain a productive research program appropriate to a major public research university.

The University of Massachusetts seeks a scholar, teacher and colleague with expertise in social interaction and culture. This is a tenure track, Assistant Professor, position. Candidates must demonstrate excellence in empirical research, with attention to linguistic diversity a strength. The person appointed will join a faculty and graduate program with distinction in ethnographic approaches to communication and comparative analysis; will add to the department's profile in international and global communication and in qualitative and interpretive methods; and will supervise and teach at all academic levels, including large undergraduate introductory courses, graduate survey and methods courses, and graduate and undergraduate seminars in the candidate's specialty.

The Department of Communication at Texas A&M University, College Station, TX, invites applications for a tenure-track position at an open rank in organizational communication. Preference will be given to senior-level applicants. Scholars with a variety of theoretical and methodological approaches are welcome, but special consideration will be given to scholars who employ quantitative research methods. We are particularly interested in applicants who specialize in discourse analysis, communication technology, organizational change and innovation, organizational knowledge, organizational identity, group communication, teams in organizations, network analysis, international or multinational organizations, and/or macro-approaches to organization communication.

The department offers the Ph.D., M.A., and B.A degrees. It has 20 tenure-track faculty members, 50 graduate students, and 800 undergraduate majors. Texas A&M University ranks in the top ten nationally in number of national merit scholars, total research expenditures, and total endowment funds.

Texas A&M University is an AA/EEO institution, is deeply committed to diversity, and responds to the needs of dual-career couples.

The Department of Communication at the University of Maryland is seeking to hire an Assistant or Associate Professor in Persuasion and Social Influence. The successful candidate will be able to teach, engage in research, and advance theory regarding quantitative approaches to persuasion and social influence. The ability to teach quantitative methods, statistical analysis, and/or mathematical modeling of communication processes is required, as is the ability to teach communication theory.
Women and minorities are particularly encouraged to apply. The University of Maryland is an Affirmative Action, Equal Employment Opportunity employer.

The Department of Communication Studies at the University of Texas at Austin invites applications for a social scientist familiar with the effects of persuasion in applied contexts. The appointment will begin in Fall. Applicants must have a Ph.D. in hand at the time of the appointment. Scholarly publications and teaching experience are preferred. The faculty member should be interested in doing field-based or experimental studies in areas such as social influence, conflict, bargaining and negotiation, or learning in health or other applied settings. Applicants with strong interests in securing and completing funded research are especially sought. The ability to teach a large undergraduate course in persuasion will be a special advantage. The University of Texas at Austin is an Equal Opportunity/Affirmative Action Employer. Minorities and women are encouraged to apply.

What is most striking in nearly all the job descriptions for positions in communication departments is the special appeal for women and persons of minority backgrounds to apply. Such persons are always "particularly encouraged to apply." We are left with the impression that these departments are genuinely committed to promoting diversity. But evidently these departments have no interest in epistemological diversity as most of the job descriptions are ONLY for persons who do quantitative research and thereby share the belief that human processes—such as communication processes—are quantifiable, observable, and measurable. Persons who are of fundamentally different epistemological persuasions are left with no opportunity to even make a case to any of these departments for a different way of studying, teaching, and understanding communication. What then does diversity mean when the only persons who can apply for many of these advertised jobs must already share the worldview of those in the departments who have the power to determine what the job description will look like, and therefore who exactly is eligible to apply?

Thirty Three

Communication &
Modern Society

As an expression of the Western/European worldview, the goal of communication studies is to produce rational human beings and ultimately help create a society that is bound by rational behaviors, principles, and processes. This worldview assumes that the rise of a rational society reflects the highest level of social, political, and economic efficiency, and, as a result, the highest point in human evolution. Supposedly, a rational human being values rigor and objectivity. From a Western/European perspective, the primary mission of education is to produce rational human beings and ultimately help sustain a *rational* society.

In communication studies, this mission can be vividly seen in how Edward Schiappa and John Nordin, authors of one of the most popular textbooks in communication studies, *Argumentation: Keeping Faith With Reason*, make the case for the study of argumentation.

This text is designed to introduce students to basic concepts in argumentation theory, criticism, and practice. Ideally, argumentation classes involve both the production and critical analysis or arguments. We live in world saturated with arguments, and to be a competent communicator requires one to be able to make a reasoned case for one's beliefs, just as it requires one to be able to judge the case set forth by others. Accordingly, we have provided students with the vocabulary and conceptual apparatus to make good arguments as well as to evaluate the arguments they are encountering.

This book is designed to be of use in the several types or classes taught involving argumentation, including those that emphasize theory and those that emphasize practice, including composition classes, oral communication classes, and introductory classes concerned with debate.

Above all, we believe that students learn the most about argumentation by actually arguing and evaluating arguments, which is why the book is heavily populated by examples and suggested exercises. Acquiring and using a vocabulary with which to describe, understand, and evaluate arguments is, we are convinced, the best way to enhance the critical thinking, speaking, and writing skills of our students.[45]

Indeed, nearly every communication curriculum has a required course that focuses on argumentation and persuasion. These courses are commonly titled *Argumentation and Decision-Making, Foundations of Persuasion and Argumentation,* and *Communication and Argumentation.*

A Syllabus

This course will identify and explain concepts you must know and the steps you must take to construct an argument. The course will emphasize argumentation as a communicative activity in which you advance claims and their grounds, then strengthen and refine them using compelling evidence so that they will resist the refutation of others.

Accordingly, the course stresses building performance skills in argumentation and public speaking. The importance of decision-making and decision makers in creating arguments will be a major theme of the course. Real-life application of the theories of argumentation will be stressed along with the importance of academic debate.

---

[45] Excerpted from Schiappa, E., & Nordin, J. (2013). *Argumentation: Keeping faith with reason.* Boston: Pearson.

Students will participate in informal debates and presentations designed to build their skills in argumentation. In addition, students will explore and enhance their personal critical thinking skills through the development of argument as well as refutation and rebuttal against arguments posed by others.

Through active participation and researched your outcomes of from this course will include:

- *Understand the characteristics of argumentation;*
- *Understand how argumentation serves critical appraisal;*
- *Identify and analyze issues;*
- *Build argumentative cases;*
- *Understand types of argument;*
- *Understand and evaluate the evidence in arguments;*
- *Understand the role of values and credibility in arguments;*
- *Develop skills to pose effective claims and to present substantive refutation and rebuttal against claims by others.*
- *Understand the role of argument spheres.*

But what is most striking about this pedagogical (teaching/learning) emphasis in communication studies on producing rational human beings is the lack of any empirical support for the many claims and objectives found in persuasion and argumentation syllabuses and textbooks.

When Facts Backfire

It's one of the great assumptions underlying modern democracy that an informed citizenry is preferable to an uninformed one. If people are furnished with the facts, they will be clearer thinkers and better citizens. If they are ignorant, facts will enlighten them. If they are mistaken, facts will set them straight.

In the end, truth will out.

Maybe not. Recently, a few political scientists have begun to discover a human tendency deeply discouraging to anyone with faith in the power of information. It's this: Facts don't necessarily have the power to change our minds. In fact, quite the opposite. In a series of studies in 2005 and 2006, researchers at the University of Michigan found that when misinformed people, particularly political partisans, were exposed to corrected facts in news stories, they rarely changed their minds. In fact, they often became even more strongly set in their beliefs. Facts, they found, were not curing misinformation. Like an underpowered antibiotic, facts could actually make misinformation even stronger.

This bodes ill for a democracy, because most voters — the people making decisions about how the country runs — aren't blank slates. They already have beliefs, and a set of facts lodged in their minds. The problem is that sometimes the things they think they know are objectively, provably false. And in the presence of the correct information, such people react very, very differently than the merely uninformed. Instead of changing their minds to reflect the correct information, they can entrench themselves even deeper.

"The general idea is that it's absolutely threatening to admit you're wrong," says political scientist Brendan Nyhan, the lead researcher on the Michigan study. The phenomenon — known as "backfire" — is "a natural defense mechanism to avoid that cognitive dissonance."

These findings open a long-running argument about the political ignorance of American citizens to broader questions about the interplay between the nature of human intelligence and our democratic ideals. Most of us like to believe that our opinions have been formed over time by careful, rational consideration of facts and ideas, and that the

*decisions based on those opinions, therefore, have the ring of sound-
ness and intelligence. In reality, we often base our opinions on our
beliefs, which can have an uneasy relationship with facts. And rather
than facts driving beliefs, our beliefs can dictate the facts we chose to
accept. They can cause us to twist facts so they fit better with our pre-
conceived notions. Worst of all, they can lead us to uncritically accept
bad information just because it reinforces our beliefs. This reinforce-
ment makes us more confident we're right, and even less likely to listen to any new information. And then we vote.*

*This effect is only heightened by the information glut, which offers —
alongside an unprecedented amount of good information — endless
rumors, misinformation, and questionable variations on the truth. In
other words, it's never been easier for people to be wrong, and at the
same time feel more certain that they're right.*

*The last five decades of political science have definitively established
that most modern-day Americans lack even a basic understanding of
how their country works. In 1996, Princeton University's Larry M.
Bartels argued, "the political ignorance of the American voter is one
of the best documented data in political science."*

*On its own, this might not be a problem: People ignorant of the facts
could simply choose not to vote. But instead, it appears that misinformed people often have some of the strongest political opinions.
A striking recent example was a study done in the year 2000, led by
James Kuklinski of the University of Illinois at Urbana-Champaign.
He led an influential experiment in which more than 1,000 Illinois
residents were asked questions about welfare — the percentage of the
federal budget spent on welfare, the number of people enrolled in the
program, the percentage of enrollees who are black, and the average
payout. More than half indicated that they were confident that their
answers were correct — but in fact only 3 percent of the people got
more than half of the questions right. Perhaps more disturbingly, the
ones who were the most confident they were right were by and large*

*the ones who knew the least about the topic. (Most of these partici-
pants expressed views that suggested a strong antiwelfare bias.)*

*Studies by other researchers have observed similar phenomena when
addressing education, health care reform, immigration, affirmative
action, gun control, and other issues that tend to attract strong par-
tisan opinion. Kuklinski calls this sort of response the "I know I'm
right" syndrome, and considers it a "potentially formidable problem"
in a democratic system. "It implies not only that most people will resist
correcting their factual beliefs," he wrote, "but also that the very people who most need to correct them will be least likely to do so."*

*What's going on? How can we have things so wrong, and be so sure
that we're right? Part of the answer lies in the way our brains are
wired. Generally, people tend to seek consistency. There is a substantial body of psychological research showing that people tend to
interpret information with an eye toward reinforcing their preex-
isting views. If we believe something about the world, we are more
likely to passively accept as truth any information that confirms our
beliefs, and actively dismiss information that doesn't. This is known
as "motivated reasoning." Whether or not the consistent information
is accurate, we might accept it as fact, as confirmation of our beliefs.
This makes us more confident in said beliefs, and even less likely to
entertain facts that contradict them.*

*New research, published in the journal Political Behavior suggests
that once those facts — or "facts" — are internalized, they are very
difficult to budge. In 2005, amid the strident calls for better media
fact-checking in the wake of the Iraq war, Michigan's Nyhan and a
colleague devised an experiment in which participants were given
mock news stories, each of which contained a provably false, though
nonetheless widespread, claim made by a political figure: that there
were WMDs found in Iraq (there weren't), that the Bush tax cuts
increased government revenues (revenues actually fell), and that the
Bush administration imposed a total ban on stem cell research (only*

certain federal funding was restricted). Nyhan inserted a clear, direct correction after each piece of misinformation, and then measured the study participants to see if the correction took.

For the most part, it didn't. The participants who self-identified as conservative believed the misinformation on WMD and taxes even more strongly after being given the correction. With those two issues, the more strongly the participant cared about the topic — a factor known as salience — the stronger the backfire. The effect was slightly different on self-identified liberals: When they read corrected stories about stem cells, the corrections didn't backfire, but the readers did still ignore the inconvenient fact that the Bush administration's restrictions weren't total.

It's unclear what is driving the behavior — it could range from simple defensiveness, to people working harder to defend their initial beliefs — but as Nyhan dryly put it, "It's hard to be optimistic about the effectiveness of fact-checking."

It would be reassuring to think that political scientists and psychologists have come up with a way to counter this problem, but that would be getting ahead of ourselves. The persistence of political misperceptions remains a young field of inquiry. "It's very much up in the air," says Nyhan.

And if you harbor the notion — popular on both sides of the aisle — that the solution is more education and a higher level of political sophistication in voters overall, well, that's a start, but not the solution. A 2006 study by Charles Taber and Milton Lodge at Stony Brook University showed that politically sophisticated thinkers were even less open to new information than less sophisticated types. These people may be factually right about 90 percent of things, but their confidence makes it nearly impossible to correct the 10 percent on which they're totally wrong. Taber and Lodge found this alarming, because engaged, sophisticated thinkers are "the very folks on whom demo-cratic theory relies most heavily."

In an ideal world, citizens would be able to maintain constant vigilance, monitoring both the information they receive and the way their brains are processing it. But keeping atop the news takes time and effort. And relentless self-questioning, as centuries of philosophers have shown, can be exhausting. Our brains are designed to create cognitive shortcuts — inference, intuition, and so forth — to avoid precisely that sort of discomfort while coping with the rush of information we receive on a daily basis. Without those shortcuts, few things would ever get done. Unfortunately, with them, we're easily suckered by political falsehoods.[46]

Persuasion & Presidents

In 1993, George Edwards, the director of the Center for Presidential Studies, at Texas A. & M. University, sponsored a program in Presidential rhetoric. The program led to a conference, and the organizers asked their patron to present a paper. Edwards didn't know anything about Presidential rhetoric himself, however, so he asked the organizers for a list of the best works in the field to help him prepare.

Like many political scientists, Edwards is an empiricist. He deals in numbers and tables and charts, and even curates something called the Presidential Data Archive. The studies he read did not impress him. One, for example, concluded that "public speech no longer attends the processes of governance—it is governance," but offered no rigorous evidence. Instead, the author justified his findings with vague statements like "One anecdote should suffice to make this latter point."

---

[46] Excerpted from Keohane, J. (2010, July 11). How facts backfire—Researchers discover a surprising threat to democracy: Our brains. *Boston Globe*. http://www.boston.com/bostonglobe/ideas/articles/2010/07/11/how_facts_backfire/?page=full

Nearly twenty years later, Edwards still sounds offended. "They were talking about Presidential speeches as if they were doing literary criticism," he says. "I just started underlining the claims that were faulty." As a result, his conference presentation, "Presidential Rhetoric: What Difference Does It Make?," was less a contribution to the research than a frontal assault on it. The paper consists largely of quotations from the other political scientists' work, followed by comments such as "He is able to offer no systematic evidence," and "We have no reason to accept such a conclusion," and "Sometimes the authors' assertions, implicit or explicit, are clearly wrong."

Edwards ended his presentation with a study of his own, on Ronald Reagan, who is generally regarded as one of the Presidency's great communicators. Edwards wrote, "If we cannot find evidence of the impact of the rhetoric of Ronald Reagan, then we have reason to reconsider the broad assumptions regarding the consequences of rhetoric." As it turns out, there was reason to reconsider. Reagan succeeded in passing major provisions of his agenda, such as the 1981 tax cuts, but, Edwards wrote, "surveys of public opinion have found that support for regulatory programs and spending on health care, welfare, urban problems, education, environmental protection and aid to minorities"—all programs that the President opposed—"increased rather than decreased during Reagan's tenure." Meanwhile, "support for increased defense expenditures was decidedly lower at the end of his administration than at the beginning." In other words, people were less persuaded by Reagan when he left office than they were when he took office.

Nor was Reagan's Presidency distinguished by an unusually strong personal connection with the electorate. A study by the Gallup organization, from 2004, found that, compared with all the Presidential job-approval ratings it had on record, Reagan's was slightly below average, at fifty-three per cent. It was only after he left office that Americans came to see him as an unusually likable and effective leader.

According to Edwards, Reagan's real achievement was to take advantage of a transformation that predated him. Edwards quotes various political scientists who found that conservative attitudes peaked, and liberal attitudes plateaued, in the late nineteen-seventies, and that Reagan was the beneficiary of these trends, rather than their instigator. Some of Reagan's closest allies support this view. Martin Anderson, who served as Reagan's chief domestic-policy adviser, wrote, "What has been called the Reagan revolution is not completely, or even mostly, due to Ronald Reagan. . . . It was the other way around." Edwards later wrote, "As one can imagine, I was a big hit with the auditorium full of dedicated scholars of rhetoric."

Edwards's views are no longer considered radical in political-science circles, in part because he has marshalled so much evidence in support of them. In his book "On Deaf Ears: The Limits of the Bully Pulpit" (2003), he expanded the poll-based rigor that he applied to Reagan's rhetorical influence to that of nearly every other President since the nineteen-thirties. Franklin Delano Roosevelt's fireside chats are perhaps the most frequently cited example of Presidential persuasion. Cue Edwards: "He gave only two or three fireside chats a year, and rarely did he focus them on legislation under consideration in Congress. It appears that FDR only used a fireside chat to discuss such matters on four occasions, the clearest example being the broadcast on March 9, 1937, on the ill-fated 'Court-packing' bill." Edwards also quotes the political scientists Matthew Baum and Samuel Kernell, who, in a more systematic examination of Roosevelt's radio addresses, found that they fostered "less than a 1 percentage point increase" in his approval rating. His more traditional speeches didn't do any better. He was unable to persuade Americans to enter the Second World War, for example, until Pearl Harbor.

No President worked harder to persuade the public, Edwards says, than Bill Clinton. Between his first inauguration, in January, 1993, and his first midterm election, in November, 1994, he travelled to nearly two hundred cities and towns, and made more than two hundred *appearances, to sell his Presidency, his legislative initiatives (notably his health-care bill), and his party. But his poll numbers fell, the health-care bill failed, and, in the next election, the Republicans took control of the House of Representatives for the first time in more than forty years. Yet Clinton never gave up on the idea that all he needed was a few more speeches, or a slightly better message. "I've got to . . . spend more time communicating with the American people," the President said in a 1994 interview. Edwards notes, "It seems never to have occurred to him or his staff that his basic strategy may have been inherently flawed."*

George W. Bush was similarly invested in his persuasive ability. After the 2004 election, the Bush Administration turned to the longtime conservative dream of privatizing Social Security. Bush led the effort, with an unprecedented nationwide push that took him to sixty cities in sixty days. "Let me put it to you this way," he said at a press conference, two days after the election. "I earned capital in the campaign, political capital, and now I intend to spend it." But the poll numbers for privatization—and for the President—kept dropping, and the Administration turned to other issues.

Obama, too, believes in the power of Presidential rhetoric. After watching the poll numbers for his health-care plan, his stimulus bill, his Presidency, and his party decline throughout 2010, he told Peter Baker, of the Times, that he hadn't done a good enough job communicating with the American people: "I think anybody who's occupied this office has to remember that success is determined by an intersection in policy and politics and that you can't be neglecting of marketing and P.R. and public opinion."

The annual State of the Union address offers the clearest example of the misconception. The best speechwriters are put on the task. The biggest policy announcements are saved for it. The speech is carried on all the major networks, and Americans have traditionally considered watching it to be something of a civic duty. And yet Gallup, after reviewing polls dating back to 1978, concluded that "these speeches rarely affect a president's public standing in a meaningful way, despite the amount of attention they receive." Obama's 2012 address fit the pattern. His approval rating was forty-six per cent on the day of the speech, and forty-seven per cent a week later.

Presidents have plenty of pollsters on staff, and they give many speeches in the course of a year. So how do they so systematically overestimate the importance of those speeches? Edwards believes that by the time Presidents reach the White House their careers have taught them that they can persuade anyone of anything. "Think about how these guys become President," he says. "The normal way is talking for two years. That's all you do, and somehow you win. You must be a really persuasive fellow."

If speeches don't make a difference, what does? Another look at the Presidencies of Franklin Roosevelt and Ronald Reagan offers an answer. Roosevelt was one of only two Presidents in the twentieth century whose parties won seats in a midterm election. That was in 1934—a year in which the economy grew by ten per cent. But in the midterms of 1938, the year after the economy plunged into a double-dip recession, the Democrats lost seventy-two seats in the House. If Roosevelt had been running for reëlection, he, too, would almost certainly have lost.

During Reagan's first two years in office, the economy fell into recession. By the time of the 1982 midterm election, unemployment had risen to 10.8 per cent and the economy had shrunk by two per cent. Already the minority party in the House, the Republicans lost twenty-six seats. Reagan's approval rating went below forty per cent. But then the economy recovered. By November, 1984, unemployment had fallen to 7.2 per cent, and the economy, remarkably, was growing at an annual rate of seven per cent. Reagan was elected to a second term in a forty-nine-state landslide.

There is no reason to believe that F.D.R.'s storytelling faltered for a single midterm election, or that Reagan lost his persuasive ability in 1982, then managed to regain it two years later. Rather, the causality appears to work the other way around: Presidents win victories because ordinary Americans feel that their lives are going well, and we call those Presidents great communicators, because their public persona is the part of them we know.[47]

Yet in the face of all of this research showing our notions of persuasion and argumentation are devoid of any foundation in reality, communication studies presses forward with the mission of cultivating "rational" beings by emphasizing persuasion and argumentation courses. Although communication studies promises to produce rational human beings who will respond positively to facts, finding mention of any of this research in communication studies is extremely difficult and often impossible. But this is what hegemony means—the ability to avoid the things that fundamentally disrupt and threaten our view of the world.

Without the notions of persuasion and argumentation, or owning up to the fact that these notions have been found to be seriously lacking in support in the real world, defending communication studies' disciplinary integrity becomes a problem for the status quo in communication studies as these notions are central to our understanding, teaching, and theorizing of communication. We would also be forced to look at what other popular notions in communication studies have no relation to reality, and how the epistemology that frames communication studies is implicated in generating and sustaining these kinds of illusory notions. Evidently, no dominant worldview would want to be subject to that kind of rigorous scrutiny. For to question an epistemology's integrity and legitimacy is to ultimately question the integrity and legitimacy of worldview that brought that epistemology—and all its related theories, pedagogies, and methodologies—into the world.

---

[47] Excerpted from Klein, E. (2012, March 19). The unpersuaded: Who listens to a President? *New Yorker.* http://www.newyorker.com/reporting/2012/03/19/120319fa_fact_klein?currentPage=all

Thirty Four

The Rise of the Machines

The goal of communication studies is to produce rational human beings and ultimately contribute to the making of a rational society—that is, the kind of society that the Western/European worldview values. This means cultivating persons who are eloquent, coherent, and have a command of communication processes that will promote rational action and decision-making. Lack of eloquence and coherence supposedly reflects a mind that is muddled, confused, and undisciplined. In communication studies, confusion presumably impedes communication, and, consequently, presumably threatens the rise of a rational society. Communication studies promises to equip us with the expertise and knowledge that will allow us to vanquish confusion, including how to use different machines to help us do so.

- *We are increasingly using machines to acquire, accumulate, and validate knowledge. New technologies are allowing us to study human beings unobtrusively. Every interaction with a technology now becomes data that could eventually be analyzed.*

- *We are increasingly using machines to gain control over various human processes that will supposedly make for a more definitive knowledge of human beings—such as the use of brain scanning technologies to understand how the human mind works.*

- *We are increasingly using machines to disseminate knowledge—smart classrooms, slide presentation technology (such as PowerPoint), virtual courses, e-learning.*

- *We are increasingly using machines to achieve the necessary knowledge that will supposedly afford success and progress—such as the rise of data-mining.*

Technology In Communication Research

Reflecting the belief that technology enables human evolution and progress, communication research is increasingly relying on technology to define and acquire communication knowledge.

SPSS (Statistical Package for the Social Sciences)
SPSS is advertised as being among the most widely used programs for statistical analysis in the social sciences. SPSS supports the analytical process with data preparation, data management, output management and charting features.

HLM (Hierarchical Linear and Nonlinear Modeling)
HLM is advertised as allowing for the study of relationships at any level in a single analysis. It claims to fit models to outcome variables and generate a linear model that accounts for variations at each level.

NUD-IST (Non-numerical Unstructured Data Indexing Searching and Theorizing)
NUD-IST is advertised as being good for simple analyses like text manuscript from focus groups or open-ended survey data to more complex theory construction and analysis. It promises to automate much of the tedious work that normally comes with qualitative data analysis by auto coding signified text data, importing table data, and using command files to regulate processes.

ATLAS-Ti
ATLAS.ti is advertised as a software program that contains tools to help the user locate, code, and annotate findings in the data, weigh and evaluate their importance, and visualize the relationships among them. It allows researchers to consolidate large volumes of documents

while keeping track of all notes, annotations, codes and memos in all fields of the data.

ETHNOGRAPH
Ethnograph is advertised as being good for researchers who need to analyze large amounts of text, including interview transcripts, field notes, open-ended surveys, etc. It is used mostly for coding and compiling patterns in data that is collected during fieldwork or from interviews.

DEDOOSE
Dedoose is advertised as a cross-platform application for analyzing text, video, and spreadsheet data (analyzing qualitative, quantitative, and mixed methods research). This "intuitive software interface" claims to allow users or teams to effectively analyze qualitative and mixed methods research data from various research approaches when conducting surveys and interviews in market research, psychology research, social science research, ethnographic research, and anthropology research.

ATLAS
Atlas is advertised as a qualitative software program that can assists researchers with the analysis of qualitative data. It promises to provide researchers with the tools to analyze, explore and share qualitative data. Its features include data management, hyperlinking, visualization, working with variables and survey importation, and illustrating links within the data and theory building.

NVivo
NVivo is advertised as a software program that supports qualitative and mixed methods research. It lets researchers collect, organize and analyze content from interviews, focus group discussions, surveys, audio, social media data, YouTube videos and web pages. It also promises to let researchers "deeply analyze" their data using powerful search, query and visualization tools.

These emerging technologies are for both quantitative and qualitative research. Indeed, all of these emerging technologies are increasingly driving communication research, making communication research easy and also abundant. Facilitating both trends (ease and abundance) is the fact that our communication is increasingly textual (texting, tweeting, emailing, facebooking), making for vast amounts of data that can be easily acquired and analyzed with these new technologies. Also aiding the vast and unsurpassed production of communication knowledge are the enormous amounts of graduates that communication programs and departments are producing and credentialing. Nearly all graduates must produce a report, thesis, or dissertation in order to graduate. We now have, by all analyses, a glut of persons with graduate degrees in communication. We also now have a glut of communication research. Our ever-increasing number of journals and annual conventions (international, national, regional, and research interests) can only accommodate a miniscule amount of all this research production. Yet even this portion is impossible for any person to read and study. Various analyses show that only a fraction of the articles in communication journals are read and even a lesser number of conference papers, theses, and dissertations are ever noticed. What then is the purpose of all this research activity and productivity? Where is the evidence that all of this research activity and productivity is improving the quality of our lives and making for a better world?

The rise of technology in communication research was long anticipated. The Western/European worldview assumes that technology improves human functioning and ultimately extends our capacity, such as improving our capacity to analyze and visualize vast amounts of data. In communication research, technology presumably allows us to identify patterns and relationships that are often invisible to the naked eye. Technology also supposedly promotes objectivity by removing human subjectivity, like our biases and prejudices. Also, technology presumably promotes precision—results and findings are always exact. In other words, technology presumably removes and lessens human error. For all these reasons the rise of technology in communication research is nearly unanimously seen as a good thing and is strongly encouraged.

But in being a human creation, technology is laden with ideology and promotes a certain ideology. The technology in communication research assumes that the human experience is observable, measurable, and quantifiable, and the experiences that lend for such processes matter the most. But, most importantly, the technology increasingly being used in communication research assumes that communication is fundamentally about human beings using signs and symbols, and consequently what should be the object of our analyses is that which is spoken and written. Simply put, the technology in communication research privileges that which is spoken and written. Only that which is spoken and written is deserving of analysis. Indeed, no technology in communication research has the capacity to analyze, visualize, and make sense of that which is never spoken and written. This is how the technology in communication research reinforces a Western/European worldview. It promotes a definition of communication that complements the epistemology that is of this worldview. It further reinforces this worldview by cultivating a communication knowledge that is amenable to the reality this worldview creates—that is, a communication knowledge that will pose no threat to this reality. Indeed, that which is unspoken and unwritten is also often about who and what is silenced and marginalized. In the end, technology contributes to the depoliticizing of communication research, or really the legitimizing of a certain kind of politics that will pose no threat to anything. In privileging that which is spoken and written the technology in communication research is also privileging those persons who have the power to speak and write without fear and threat of recrimination and punishment, and consequently have the power to dictate what is good, moral, and decent. This, again, is how worldviews are self-reinforcing and self-perpetuating.

Thirty Five

Technology, Epistemology & Communication

> New technologies are increasingly shaping our communication practices and behaviors in ways that compromise the rigors and demands of communication. Regardless of how differently we define communication, communication requires time, patience, and perseverance. New technologies release us of these demands. We now mistake connecting for communicating. According to Sherry Turkle, a psychologist and professor at MIT, *"In conversation we tend to one another. We can attend to tone and nuance. In conversation, we are called upon to see things from another's point of view."* Moreover, face-to-face conversation *"teaches patience. When we communicate on our digital devices, we learn different habits. As we ramp up the volume and velocity of online connections, we start to expect faster answers. To get these, we ask one another simpler questions; we dumb down our communications, even on the most important matters."* Finally, through conversation with others we *"learn to converse with ourselves. So our flight from conversation can mean diminished chances to learn skills of self-reflection. These days, social media continually asks us what's "on our mind," but we have little motivation to say something truly self-reflective. Self-reflection in*

conversation requires trust. It's hard to do anything with 3,000 Facebook friends except connect."[48]

➤ New technologies are increasingly moving us away from the real world (to virtual worlds), thereby undermining the development of the temperament that is vital to dealing with the demands of the real world. In the real world, for instance, difficult human beings cannot simply be erased or blocked. We have to devise ways to live and work with these people, and this is often difficult and demanding.

➤ New technologies are enabling the production of a knowledge that is devoid of confusion and complexity. The abstract nature of this knowledge distorts our reality.

Recognizing The Enemy

WASHINGTON — Gen. Stanley A. McChrystal, the leader of American and NATO forces in Afghanistan, was shown a PowerPoint slide in Kabul last summer that was meant to portray the complexity of American military strategy, but looked more like a bowl of spaghetti.

"When we understand that slide, we'll have won the war," General McChrystal dryly remarked, one of his advisers recalled, as the room erupted in laughter.

The slide has since bounced around the Internet as an example of a military tool that has spun out of control. Like an insurgency, PowerPoint has crept into the daily lives of military commanders and reached the level of near obsession. The amount of time expended on PowerPoint, the Microsoft presentation program of computer-generated charts, graphs and bullet points, has made it a running joke in the Pentagon and in Iraq and Afghanistan.

---

[48] Turkle, S. (2012, April 21). The flight from conversation. *New York Times*. http://www.nytimes.com/2012/04/22/opinion/sunday/the-flight-from-conversation.html

"PowerPoint makes us stupid," Gen. James N. Mattis of the Marine Corps, the Joint Forces commander, said this month at a military conference in North Carolina. (He spoke without PowerPoint.) Brig. Gen. H. R. McMaster, who banned PowerPoint presentations when he led the successful effort to secure the northern Iraqi city of Tal Afar in 2005, followed up at the same conference by likening PowerPoint to an internal threat.

"It's dangerous because it can create the illusion of understanding and the illusion of control," General McMaster said in a telephone interview afterward. "Some problems in the world are not bullet-izable."

In General McMaster's view, PowerPoint's worst offense is not a chart like the spaghetti graphic, which was first uncovered by NBC's Richard Engel, but rigid lists of bullet points (in, say, a presentation on a conflict's causes) that take no account of interconnected political, economic and ethnic forces. "If you divorce war from all of that, it becomes a targeting exercise," General McMaster said.

Commanders say that behind all the PowerPoint jokes are serious concerns that the program stifles discussion, critical thinking and thoughtful decision-making. Not least, it ties up junior officers — referred to as PowerPoint Rangers — in the daily preparation of slides, be it for a Joint Staff meeting in Washington or for a platoon leader's pre-mission combat briefing in a remote pocket of Afghanistan.

Last year when a military Web site, Company Command, asked an Army platoon leader in Iraq, Lt. Sam Nuxoll, how he spent most of his time, he responded, "Making PowerPoint slides." When pressed, he said he was serious.

"I have to make a storyboard complete with digital pictures, diagrams and text summaries on just about anything that happens," Lieutenant Nuxoll told the Web site. "Conduct a key leader engagement? Make a storyboard. Award a microgrant? Make a storyboard."

Despite such tales, "death by PowerPoint," the phrase used to described the numbing sensation that accompanies a 30-slide briefing, seems here to stay. The program, which first went on sale in 1987 and was acquired by Microsoft soon afterward, is deeply embedded in a military culture that has come to rely on PowerPoint's hierarchical ordering of a confused world.

"There's a lot of PowerPoint backlash, but I don't see it going away anytime soon," said Capt. Crispin Burke, an Army operations officer at Fort Drum, N.Y

Gen. David Petraeus, who oversees the wars in Iraq and Afghanistan and says that sitting through some PowerPoint briefings is "just agony," nonetheless likes the program for the display of maps and statistics showing trends. He has also conducted more than a few PowerPoint presentations himself.

General McChrystal gets two PowerPoint briefings in Kabul per day, plus three more during the week. General Mattis, despite his dim view of the program, said a third of his briefings are by PowerPoint.

Commanders say that the slides impart less information than a five-page paper can hold, and that they relieve the briefer of the need to polish writing to convey an analytic, persuasive point.[49]

---

[49] Excerpted from Bumiller, E. (2010, April 26). We have met the enemy and he is PowerPoint. *New York Times.* http://www.nytimes.com/2010/04/27/world/27powerpoint.html?_r=0

➤ New technologies are increasingly turning us into machines. We increasingly have networks rather than relationships, hook-ups rather than relationships, information specialists rather than producers. *"We've become,"* according to Sherry Turkle, *"accustomed to a new way of being alone together. Technology-enabled, we are able to be with one another, and also elsewhere, connected to wherever we want to be. We want to customize our lives. We want to move in and out of where we are because the thing we value most is control over where we focus our attention. We have gotten used to the idea of being in a tribe of one, loyal to our own party."*

Thirty Six

Epistemology &
Technology

We are yet to come to terms with the fact that to use a technology is to be shaped by that technology. What this relationship means is that technology is always political and ideological. Different technologies come with different social consequences and implications.

The Future Is Now

I think it is no exaggeration to say we are on the cusp of the further perfection of extreme evil, an evil whose possibility spreads well beyond that which weapons of mass destruction bequeathed to the nation-states, on to a surprising and terrible empowerment of extreme individuals.

Perhaps it is always hard to see the bigger impact while you are in the vortex of a change. Failing to understand the consequences of our inventions while we are in the rapture of discovery and innovation seems to be a common fault of scientists and technologists; we have long been driven by the overarching desire to know that is the nature of science's quest, not stopping to notice that the progress to newer and more powerful technologies can take on a life of its own.

Technologies such as human cloning have in particular raised our awareness of the profound ethical and moral issues we face. If, for example, we were to reengineer ourselves into several separate and unequal species using the power of genetic engineering, then we would threaten the notion of equality that is the very cornerstone of our democracy.

The enabling breakthrough to assemblers seems quite likely within the next 20 years. Molecular electronics - the new subfield of nanotechnology where individual molecules are circuit elements - should mature quickly and become enormously lucrative within this decade, causing a large incremental investment in all nanotechnologies.

Unfortunately, as with nuclear technology, it is far easier to create destructive uses for nanotechnology than constructive ones. Nanotechnology has clear military and terrorist uses, and you need not be suicidal to release a massively destructive nanotechnological device - such devices can be built to be selectively destructive, affecting, for example, only a certain geographical area or a group of people who are genetically distinct.

An immediate consequence of the Faustian bargain in obtaining the great power of nanotechnology is that we run a grave risk - the risk that we might destroy the biosphere on which all life depends.

It is most of all the power of destructive self-replication in genetics, nanotechnology, and robotics (GNR) that should give us pause. Self-replication is the modus operandi of genetic engineering, which uses the machinery of the cell to replicate its designs, and the prime danger underlying gray goo in nanotechnology. Stories of run-amok robots like the Borg, replicating or mutating to escape from the ethical constraints imposed on them by their creators, are well established in our science fiction books and movies.

It is even possible that self-replication may be more fundamental than we thought, and hence harder - or even impossible - to control. In truth, we have had in hand for years clear warnings of the dangers inherent in widespread knowledge of GNR technologies - of the possibility of knowledge alone enabling mass destruction. But these warnings haven't been widely publicized; the public discussions have been clearly inadequate. There is no profit in publicizing the dangers.

The nuclear, biological, and chemical (NBC) technologies used in 20th-century weapons of mass destruction were and are largely military, developed in government laboratories. In sharp contrast, the 21st-century GNR technologies have clear commercial uses and are being developed almost exclusively by corporate enterprises. In this age of triumphant commercialism, technology - with science as its handmaiden - is delivering a series of almost magical inventions that are the most phenomenally lucrative ever seen. We are aggressively pursuing the promises of these new technologies within the now-unchallenged system of global capitalism and its manifold financial incentives and competitive pressures.

This is the first moment in the history of our planet when any species, by its own voluntary actions, has become a danger to itself - as well as to vast numbers of others.

It might be a familiar progression, transpiring on many worlds - a planet, newly formed, placidly revolves around its star; life slowly forms; a kaleidoscopic procession of creatures evolves; intelligence emerges which, at least up to a point, confers enormous survival value; and then technology is invented. It dawns on them that there are such things as laws of Nature, that these laws can be revealed by experiment, and that knowledge of these laws can be made both to save and to take lives, both on unprecedented scales. Science, they recognize, grants immense powers. In a flash, they create world-altering contrivances. Some planetary civilizations see their way through,

209

place limits on what may and what must not be done, and safely pass through the time of perils. Others, not so lucky or so prudent, perish.

We should have learned a lesson from the making of the first atomic bomb and the resulting arms race. We didn't do well then, and the parallels to our current situation are troubling.[50]

Fear of The Machines

Impressed and alarmed by advances in artificial intelligence, a group of computer scientists is debating whether there should be limits on research that might lead to loss of human control over computer-based systems that carry a growing share of society's workload, from waging war to chatting with customers on the phone.

Their concern is that further advances could create profound social disruptions and even have dangerous consequences.

As examples, the scientists pointed to a number of technologies as diverse as experimental medical systems that interact with patients to simulate empathy, and computer worms and viruses that defy extermination and could thus be said to have reached a "cockroach" stage of machine intelligence.

While the computer scientists agreed that we are a long way from Hal, the computer that took over the spaceship in "2001: A Space Odyssey," they said there was legitimate concern that technological progress would transform the work force by destroying a widening range of jobs, as well as force humans to learn to live with machines that increasingly copy human behaviors.

The researchers — leading computer scientists, artificial intelligence researchers and roboticists who met at the Asilomar Conference Grounds on Monterey Bay in California — generally discounted the possibility of highly centralized superintelligences and the idea that

---

[50] Excerpted from Joy, B. Why the future doesn't need us: Our most powerful 21st-century technologies - robotics, genetic engineering, and nanotech - are threatening to make humans an endangered species. *Wired.* http://www.wired.com/wired/archive/8.04/joy_pr.html

intelligence might spring spontaneously from the Internet. But they agreed that robots that can kill autonomously are either already here or will be soon.

They focused particular attention on the specter that criminals could exploit artificial intelligence systems as soon as they were developed. What could a criminal do with a speech synthesis system that could masquerade as a human being? What happens if artificial intelligence technology is used to mine personal information from smart phones? The researchers also discussed possible threats to human jobs, like self-driving cars, software-based personal assistants and service robots in the home.

The meeting on the future of artificial intelligence was organized by Eric Horvitz, a Microsoft researcher who is now president of the association.

Dr. Horvitz said he believed computer scientists must respond to the notions of superintelligent machines and artificial intelligence systems run amok.

The idea of an "intelligence explosion" in which smart machines would design even more intelligent machines was proposed by the mathematician I. J. Good in 1965. Later, in lectures and science fiction novels, the computer scientist Vernor Vinge popularized the notion of a moment when humans will create smarter-than-human machines, causing such rapid change that the "human era will be ended." He called this shift the Singularity.[51]

---

[51] Excerpted from Markoff, J. (2009, July 25). Scientists worry machines may outsmart man. *New York Times*. http://www.nytimes.com/2009/07/26/science/26robot.html?_r=0

Thirty Seven

Illusions of the Rational Subject

Yet for all our determination to produce rational human beings and ultimately a rational society, economists and psychologists can point to no compelling results or findings that show us becoming increasingly rational, logical, and analytical. We merely have the illusion of being rational. We still do many things that are contrary to being rational.

- ➤ *Negativity seduction*. We tend to focus on the bad, remember the bad, and are most influenced by bad situations and experiences. The bad crowds out the good.
- ➤ *Focusing illusion*. We tend to focus on things that matter to us rather than what matters to others.
- ➤ *Loss aversion*. We make decisions based on avoiding loss rather than achieving gains. We tend to choose safety and avoid risks.
- ➤ *Illusion of control*. We tend to attribute our success to skill and temperament rather than luck and circumstances.
- ➤ *Optimism bias & planning fallacy*. We tend to overestimate what we know. We also tend to exaggerate our ability to forecast the future. We tend to view our attributes more positively than they really are.

➢ *Illusion of validity*. We tend to view our conclusions as always right.

➢ *Halo effect*. We tend to attach personality attributes to the success of an organization. So a winning coach is a visionary. He does everything well. Who calls a losing coach a visionary?

➢ *Illusion of understanding*. We tend to believe that we understand the past correctly. We presumably know why things happened. We therefore tend to exaggerate our own ability to understand the present and future.

➢ *Illusion of causation*. We tend to get the relationship between causes and effects completely wrong.

➢ *The anchoring effect*. We tend to let numbers, prices, and figures shape our view of reality.[52]

---

[52] These points are fully discussed in Kahneman, D. (2011). *Thinking, fast and slow*. New York: Farrar, Straus and Giroux.

Thirty Eight

Different Definitions of Communication

Definitions matter. How we define something will shape how we perceive and make sense of something. In other words, how we define something will guide how we create knowledge of that thing. Also, how we define something is about who gets to define things. That is, how we define something is about which worldview will dictate our knowledge of that something. Finally, how we define something will reinforce many other things we already believe, and thereby provide much more coherence to our worldview.

Most of the knowledge that forms the foundation of communication studies is of the definition that communication is a linguistic and symbolic process that enables the sharing of our thoughts and emotions. As Klaus Krippendorff, Emeritus Professor of Communication at the University of Pennsylvania, notes, *"the idea that communication consists of sending discreet messages from one place to another and that messages contain something, thoughts, information, instructions, meanings, feelings, etc. permeates everyday accounts of language and communication and, I would add, dominates the language of communication research as well."*[53] The theories, pedagogies, methodologies, and technologies that guide and shape communication studies are all

---

[53] Krippendorff, K. (1993). Major metaphors of communication and some Constructive Reflections on their use. *Cybernetics & Human Knowing, 2* (1), 3-5.

born of this definition of communication, and, consequently, reinforce and perpetuate the worldview that gives this definition life. This is how hegemony behaves. Who controls how we define communication also controls how we study and teach something. To study communication from this definition of communication is to study how we use language and symbols to create, exchange, and manipulate messages. Presumably, the purpose of communication is to share our thoughts and emotions with others, and this is achieved by removing confusion. Although many different versions of this definition of communication are found in communication textbooks and discourses, all share the same premises.

Communication is any act by which one person gives to or receives from another person information about that person's needs, desires, perceptions, knowledge, or affective states.

Communication is a social process in which individuals employ symbols to establish and interpret meaning in their environment.

Communication is the exchange and interpretation of signs and symbols between (and within) human agents in search of understanding.

Communication is a process in which people interact with each other by using symbols to achieve understanding.

Communication is the ability to express yourself effectively through language and gestures.

Communication is the process of creating, expressing and receiving meanings through sets of codes.

Communication is the interaction through various forms of mediums.

Communication is the avenue, channel, or process in which we are able to construct, define, persuade, and project our interests, beliefs, ideas and actions to our community.

But no worldview is capable of achieving and sustaining a perfect hege-mony. There are always places of dissent, conflict, tension, and even revolt. These places exist in communication studies and can be found in different definitions of communication situated on the margins of communication studies.

> There are definitions of communication that view communica-tion in terms of relationships. Communication is a relationship-creating, relationship-sustaining, relationship-undermining activity. To study communication from this definition is to study how we create, compromise, and navigate relationships. The purpose of communication is to shape ourselves relation-ally rather than individually. We become what our relation-ships become.

> There are definitions of communication that view communica-tion in terms of meaning. Communication is a meaning-creat-ing, meaning-sustaining, meaning-destroying activity. To study communication from this definition is to study how we create, negotiate, and validate meaning. The purpose of communica-tion is to make sense of our world, each other, and ourselves. We emancipate ourselves by emancipating our meaning-cre-ation processes.

> There are definitions of communication that view communica-tion in terms of being. Communication is about being vulnerable to the humanity of others. To study communication from this definition is to study how we create ourselves and our worlds by how we engage and relate to ourselves and each other. The purpose of communication is to enlarge our sense of possibility. By extending our capacity to be vulnerable we enlarge what we are capable of imagining and becoming.

These different definitions of communication reflect different ways of studying, theorizing, and teaching communication. These defini-tions also represent different social and political consequences. Each definition presents a different story about the relationship between communication and the human condition. Also, each definition presents a different vision of what is possible and what the world can potentially become. Hegemony means that all the different visions that these different definitions of communication present will remain marginalized in the teaching, studying, and theorizing of communication. We will be left with the impression that there is only one way to study and teach communication. Such again is how hegemony behaves and why definitions matter.

The study of communication should begin at the definitional level. Yes, *how* is communication being defined and by *whom* are no doubt important questions. But there are many other questions that matter in determining the value and capacity of any proposed definition.

➢ *How is communication achieved in this definition of communication?*
➢ *What is being assumed in this definition of communication about the relation between communication and the human condition?*
➢ *What is being valued in this definition of communication?*
➢ *How is communication undermined in this definition of communication?*
➢ *What is the purpose of communication in this definition of communication?*
➢ *What is the value of communication in this definition of communication?*
➢ *What constitutes communication knowledge in this definition of communication?*
➢ *Why should this knowledge be sought? Or, why is this knowledge presumably important?*
➢ *Who is this knowledge important to?*

Thirty Nine

Implications & Definitions

I. Every different definition of communication has different disci-
    plinary origins and associations.

    ➤ A language and symbols approach to communication tends
      to be associated with psychology. In many cases the goal is to
      identify underlying psychological processes shaping communi-
      cation behaviors.

    ➤ A meaning approach to communication tends to be associ-
      ated with sociology and anthropology. In many cases the goal
      is to understand how society is shaping our meaning-making
      processes.

    ➤ A relational approach to communication tends to be associated
      with social psychology. The goal in many cases is to understand
      the relation between social and relational forces and our psy-
      chological wellbeing.

    ➤ A being approach to communication tends to be associated with
      social psychology, sociology, anthropology, and theology. The
      goal in many cases is to identify *all* the forces that bear on our
      understanding and experiencing of things.

II. Every definition has different ambitions and aspirations. That is, every definition aspires to understand something different.

   ➤ A language and symbols approach aspires to know how best to effectively and efficiently transmit, convey, and transfer our meanings and messages.

   ➤ A meaning approach aspires to understand how different peoples make meanings, value meanings, and share meanings.

   ➤ A relational approach aspires to understand what kinds of communication practices make for different kinds of relationships.

   ➤ A being approach aspires to understand the rhetorical and communicational practices that can enlarge all that human beings are capable of understanding and experiencing.

III. Every definition speaks to a different vision of the human condition.

   ➤ A language and symbols approach tends to focus on psychological/biological forces.

   ➤ A meaning approach tends to focus on cultural forces.

   ➤ A relational approach tends to focus on social and relational forces.

   ➤ A being approach tends to focus on ecological and theological forces.

IV. Every definition implicates a different set of ethics and politics.

   ➤ A language and symbols approach focuses on using language and symbols properly. Viewing communication in terms of language and symbols makes for an ethics that stresses utility and functionality. Ethics is about using language and symbols in ways that promote harmony. Using language and symbols in ways offend people is assumed to be wrong. Using language and symbols in ways that allow for abuse and exploitation of others is also assumed to be wrong.

   ➤ A meaning approach focuses on discouraging the suppression of meaning. That is, viewing communication in terms of

meaning makes for an ethics that promotes creating and sharing meaning. We are to avoid practices that suppress the creation of meaning.

> A relational approach focuses on discouraging anything that
undermines relationships. In other words, to view communication in terms of relationships makes for an ethics that promotes
empathy, honesty, and transparency—the elements that make
for constructive relationships.

> A being approach focuses on discouraging anything impedes
the emancipation of the spirit. That is, viewing communication
in terms of being makes for an ethics that promotes the expansion and evolution of being. Such an ethics is against practices,
structures, and arrangements that limit what a human being is
capable of becoming, experiencing, and understanding, assuming of course that reaching for such modes of being poses no
threat to the well-being of others.

V. Every definition lends for a different communication knowledge.
That is, every definition employs and lends for different theories,
pedagogies, and methodologies.

> A language and symbols approach generally aims to produce a
knowledge that will increase our functionality and productivity. The goal is to produce a knowledge that will help us solve
problems and be more productive and effective. Persons who
approach communication from this perspective are generally interested in theories and methodologies that allow us to
predict and control human processes. Thus theories and methodologies that promise to reveal the workings of our biological and psychological processes—like Uncertainty Reduction
Theory, Expectations Theory, Cognitive Dissonance Theory,
Action Assembly Theory, and Communication Accommodation
Theory—are especially valued.

> A meaning approach to communication generally aspires to
produce a knowledge that will reveal how social and cultural

forces affect meaning-creation processes. This approach tends to be interested in theories—like Symbolic Interaction Theory, Structuration Theory, and Social Learning Theory—and methodologies that promise thick and rich descriptions of these processes.

➤ A relational approach to communication is also interested in theories and methodologies that promise rich and thick descriptions rather than those that promise to help us predict and control human processes. In this case, however, the goal is to produce a knowledge of human beings as relational beings, in the hope that such a knowledge will make for a society that values relationships rather individuals.

➤ A being approach to communication is generally interested in the development of epistemological resources that will reveal how and what forces impede the emancipation of being. The focus is epistemological rather than theoretical or methodological, as communication is assumed to be bound up with epistemology. How we perceive and make sense of things influences how we relate and communicate to things. In a being approach the focus is on a knowledge that comes about through self-reflection—that is, looking at how our epistemological standpoint is shaping what we are understanding and experiencing.

VI. Finally, every definition of communication reflects a different way of defining what it means to study communication.

➤ A person who views communication from a language and symbols perspective would possibly say, *"I study how we use language and symbols to create, exchange, and manipulate messages to achieve various goals and navigate different situations and challenges."*

➤ A person who views communication from a meaning perspective would possibly say, *"I study how we create, negotiate, and validate what things mean."*

➤ A person who views communication from a relationship perspective would possibly say, *"I study how we create, compromise, and navigate relationships by our communication behavior."*

➤ A person who views communication from a being perspective would possibly say, *"I study how we create ourselves and our worlds by how we engage and relate to ourselves and each other."*

Forty

Criticisms of the Status Quo in Communication Studies

There is a status quo in communication studies. A status quo is what passes for a natural order. It is defined as the existing state of affairs. The status quo in communication studies assumes that there is a certain way to study, teach, and embody communication. But there are criticisms of the status quo in communication studies that need to be noted.

> ➤ The status quo in communication studies assumes that there is no relation between communication and human condition, nor is there any between communication and the condition of the world. Supposedly, communication is merely an evolutionary tool that facilitates the sharing of our thoughts and emotions. But there is a profound relation between communication and the human condition—communication ends isolation and isolation destroys the human condition.

> ➤ The status quo in communication studies locates meaning in language and symbols. Thus we see the rise of speech codes and calls to end the use of various words. Certain words are assumed

to be inherently offensive. But to locate meaning in words is to remove from human beings the power to shape and determine what words and symbols mean.

➤ The status quo in communication studies promotes narcissism by privileging the person who is speaking and writing. Being an effective communicator is supposedly about the ability to convey our thought and emotions eloquently and effectively. The other person is merely the object of our communication. Yet how much of our communication problems begin and end with listening rather than speaking?

➤ The status quo in communication studies promotes assimilation and undermines human diversity. If communication is a symbolic and linguistic process, then sharing a common language becomes necessary for communication. Yet there is no case in history that shows that language diversity impedes peace and prosperity.

➤ The status quo in communication studies reinforces a worldview of war and conflict. The theories, pedagogies, technologies, and methodologies that form the foundation of communication studies assume that confusion is the antithesis of communication. We must strive to vanquish confusion. Communication presumably comes from our conquest of confusion. This equation makes for a never-ending conflict with confusion, as confusion simply cannot be removed from human affairs.

The Reasons Being

✓ Confusion comes from language. What words and symbols mean is always changing. Also, what words and symbols mean is determined and shaped by context, and context has many different dimensions (e.g., relational, cultural, historical, ideological).

✓ Confusion comes from human beings. We will never fully know what we mean or may mean as our experiences are always changing.

✓ Confusion comes from life. As our life unfolds, our meanings tend to change. We are also susceptible to life-altering incidents that change what things mean.

✓ Confusion comes from the world. The world is bound by limits (24 hours a day, 7 days a week, 15 weeks a semester, 12 months a year). Thus our ability to know what others mean is always scant, cursory, and limited as our experiences with others are always scant, cursory, and limited due to temporal constraints. This reality encourages us to make various impressions and perceptions of people that are usually wrong, and this often creates confusion.

Forty One

The New Colonialism

In quantitative research and much of qualitative research, the goal is to maintain separation between those conducting the research and those under study so that observations are seen to be devoid of bias and prejudice. We value and promote detachment. Detachment usually comes in the form of us bringing various theories to bear on various realities so as to give the impression that it is our theories rather than us that are doing the describing. Our goal is to have our theories illuminate the underlying order that is supposedly inherent in these realities. In this way, theories operate as a kind of torchlight: the more powerful a theory, the more it presumably illuminates. We therefore aspire to develop more and more powerful theories. We are all theorists now. In the physical sciences the goal is to develop a theory that will illuminate everything, one that will allow us, to use Stephen Hawking's words, to even know the mind of God. Although in communication studies our goal is less grand, our attitude is the same. We believe that theories objectively describe and illuminate underlying processes. However, theories do nothing of the sort.

> Politically, the more territory a theory covers, the more it is preferred, the better it will be remembered, and the more likely it will be applied. Thus, theorizing supports a conceptual imperialism: the urge to oversee, predict, control, and govern ever-growing territories—an inkling that science shares with other forms of government in national, spiritual, or commercial spheres of life. True, theories by themselves neither reign nor rule. Once institutionalized, however, they do encourage

*their users to "survey," "capture," "represent," "monitor," and ulti-
mately "manage." (p. 4)*[54]

Detachment is about creating the impression that the theory—rather
than us—is doing the illuminating and describing. We are merely
observing and recording what the theory is illuminating and describing.
But in reality we are doing the illuminating and describing as a theory
is a human creation, and choosing a theory and determining how that
theory will be used are both human processes.

*Theories are not merely found. They are constructed, proposed, pro-
moted, published, discussed, and either adopted or rejected. Their
reality lies in stating them, in understanding them as such, and in
enacting them into actual practice. These are the acts of real people,
actors who see some virtue in promulgating what they speak of. It
follows that that theorizing cannot be understood from a notion of
language as a neutral medium of representations . . . or from the cor-
ollary that theories can be justifiable by observations (of objects outside language) only. From this perspective, theories cannot be found
in the statements or inside individual minds; rather, they are discovered in processes of their continuous rearticulations. Theories that
fail to compel people to reproduce, to recirculate them within their
community, simply fade away. (pp. 6-7)*[55]

Our theories can only illuminate and describe the world we already
assume and imagine. No theory can describe a world that has no relation to the world that brought that theory into being. To theorize is to
believe. Theorizing is about affirming the world we assume and imagine. This is how theorizing promotes colonialism. Theorizing gives the
impression that our theories are illuminating and describing a world
that is outside and separate from us. The nature and features of this
world—like gravity—are presumably true for all human beings. But this
is false. Every worldview gives us a different vision of the world that

---

[54] Krippendorff, K. (2000). *On the Otherness that Theory creates.* http://repository.
upenn.edu/cgi/viewcontent.cgi?article=1310&context=asc_papers
[55] Krippendorff, K. (2000). *On the Otherness that Theory creates.* http://repository.
upenn.edu/cgi/viewcontent.cgi?article=1310&context=asc_papers

emphasizes certain features and deemphasizes other. In other words, what gravity means to us and why gravity matters to us can be absent in a different worldview. Without our meanings the world's various features mean nothing.

Detachment also means that there shall be no communication between those doing the studying and those under study, or at least no communication that can fundamentally alter anything in the study. Those under study are silenced and disenfranchised. Power exclusively resides within the hands of those doing the research and conducting the study. Only those persons with the supposed expertise to do research and make knowledge will determine which theories will be used and how the observations will be described and analyzed. Those under study will have no involvement in these processes. Nor will they have any involvement in what becomes of this research or how this research will be used to make knowledge and eventually shape public policy.

Detachment promotes hierarchy. It gives power to an exclusive few and disenfranchises the majority. It also fosters the belief that this power rightfully belongs to this exclusive few by their presumable possession of a certain expertise that is both difficult to come by and also highly valued in our society. Presumably, those under study, by lacking knowledge of the theorizing process, are incapable of making any profound sense of anything, or at least any that is comparable to any made by those with expertise of theory.

All of this makes for a certain kind of epistemological hubris, or epistemological imperialism, or epistemological chauvinism. We believe that our theories make for a superior knowledge of the world, and that having a command of theories make for a legitimate expertise that is deserving of an elevated status in our society. We also believe that our prosperity resides in developing more and more powerful theories, and investing in the technologies that will help us derive these theories. We therefore believe that education should be about acquiring a command of theories and also learning how to employ theories.

We struggle to appreciate other ways of making sense of the world. There are presumably no stories comparable to our theories. We have no qualms asking which story would have put a human being on the moon.

That there are presumably no stories comparable to our own theories means that no other civilization has an epistemology comparable to our own. Ours is supposedly the best—a product of the "finest minds" and the "finest institutions." This is, after all, the epistemology that the rest of the world is now seeking to adopt. Thus we believe that safeguarding the integrity of this epistemology is imperative. We believe that this begins with upholding our standards of academic excellence.

In the face of all of this epistemological imperialism, epistemological diversity becomes impossible. We have no foundation for this kind of diversity. The most that can be had is a diversity that poses no threat to anything. This is the only diversity we can embrace.

The problem with the status quo in communication studies is the absence of any *epistemological generosity*—a way of understanding the world that genuinely promotes consideration of different worldviews. Epistemological generosity means removing the hegemony of our theories, pedagogies, and methodologies. It means releasing ourselves of the illusion that our meanings and understandings objectively reflect a world that is outside and separate from us. It means coming to terms with the fact that our theories, pedagogies, and methodologies are human creations, reflecting our own fears and ambitions. Our world is of our own making. Epistemological generosity is about our dismantling all the devices that mask our vulnerability—the vulnerability that comes with being human.

Communication studies also reflects a lack *epistemological imagination*—lacking the ability to reimagine what communication can be. Nothing is inherently wrong with using a certain epistemology, or a certain set of theories and methodologies, to understand communication. The problem is when a certain epistemology is so dominant that it displaces other epistemologies, blocks the rise of new epistemologies, and is even openly hostile to different epistemologies. The problem is particularly debilitating when this dominant epistemology forwards a narrow view of communication that impoverishes our sense of wonder and imagination.

The hegemony of the Western/European epistemology in communication studies, by controlling most of the levers of power and privilege in communication studies, is impeding our reimagining of communication. When we are unable to enlarge our sense of wonder and imagination, we lose that which most makes us human. We become what we imagine. We therefore gain nothing by impeding our sense of wonder and imagination.

Forty Two

On the Rise of New Worldviews

Because every worldview is self-reinforcing, self-perpetuating, and self-legitimizing, and a dominant worldview controls the levers of influence and privilege, toppling a dominant worldview is difficult. It is also nearly impossible to change a worldview from the inside as each component of a worldview (ontology, epistemology, and axiology) sustains the other components. Instead, history reveals that new worldviews come about by other means.

I. A new worldview emerges when a violent disruption (natural or human) shatters the institutional foundation of the dominant worldview.

II. A new worldview emerges when the social, political, ideological, economical, and cultural conditions that support the current worldview change.

III. A new worldview emerges when the dominant worldview can no longer fulfill its promises and people begin to lose faith in it.

The world is now witnessing the coming of a new worldview. The hegemony of the Western/European worldview is slowly imploding. The world is becoming racially different, technologically different, economically different, politically different, and religiously different in ways that demand new kinds of thinking. Old orders and institutions are collapsing under the weight of this transformation and slowly giving way to new orders and institutions. This emerging world is demanding new definitions of communication that can deal with our exploding diversity and complexity, as well as all the issues and concerns that come with a world where we must recognize that our own fates are bound up with the fates of all others who share this planet with us. A new worldview will make for a new epistemology of communication that will bring new theories/stories, pedagogies, and methodologies of communication that complement this emerging world.

Forty Three

On the End of
Colonialism

So what now is the moral of the story? What becomes of a civilization that politically, ideologically, and epistemologically aspires to conquer every dimension of the world? That is, what becomes of a civilization—or any civilization—that views conquest as the path to progress and prosperity? History will record that such a civilization will end badly. History will also record that colonization is contrary to the world's natural order and rhythms and, in being so, will make for only misery and death. Indeed, history will record that the negative effects of colonization are many, and all in one way or another will fall back on us.

I. Our quest to impose our worldview on other civilizations—such as under the banner of promoting democracy, progress, and prosperity—makes for the loss of human diversity through the loss of cultures, languages, and civilizations.

Language Diversity Matters

The United Nations Education and Scientific Organization (UNESCO) recently produced a report that focuses on "the need to recognize that linguistic diversity is a treasure contributing to human knowledge and to the many different ways of gaining access to knowledge" (p.

154). Acknowledging the fact that many persons view linguistic diversity as an obstacle to development, the report contends that "It is crucial to recognize that linguistic diversity is a source of enrichment for humanity and cannot be seen as a handicap when it is combined with cultural diversity" (p. 154). As such, "The disappearance of a language is a loss for all human beings for it generally means the disappearance not only of a way of life and a culture, but also a representation of the world and of an often unique form of access to knowledge and to the mind" (p. 154).

The UNESCO report discusses various reasons as to why preserving and promoting linguistic diversity is vital. For instance, such diversity is important for cognitive ergonomics. "Indeed to set limits on linguistic diversity in knowledge societies would be tantamount to reducing the paths of access to knowledge, since their capacity to adapt technically, cognitively and culturally to the needs of their actual or potential users would be diminished. Preserving the plurality of languages translates into enabling the largest number to have access to the media of knowledge" (p. 153). Moreover, linguistic diversity preserves indigenous languages, which "play an essential role in national construction." The report claims that "Indigenous languages continue to be the main medium of expression of aspirations, intimate desires, feelings, and local life. They are indeed the repositories of cultures" (p. 152).

In order to preserve and promote linguistic diversity, UNESCO recommends that school systems throughout the world "encourage the expansion, within pluralistic education communities, of a multilingual culture, reconciling the requirements of the teaching of a mother tongue and of several other languages" (p. 154). It also calls for educational systems that are bilingual, and where resources permit, even trilingual. "This policy could be facilitated by massive exchanges of teachers and language assistants within the region of the world, or indeed between regions" (p. 154). Besides introducing peoples to different knowledge systems, UNESCO also points to the fact "that bilingual persons usually possess a greater cognitive malleability and flexibility than do monolingual persons." In this way, all peoples stand to gain from the preservation and promotion of linguistic diversity. According to UNESCO, "Reducing the erosion of linguistic diversity, discovering ways to prevent the fast extinction of indigenous languages or promoting the wide use of several common languages, does not mean championing a lost cause for the sake of nostalgia. It means, rather, an acknowledgement that languages are at once cognitive media, vehicles of culture and an enabling environment for knowledge societies, for which diversity and pluralism are synonymous with enrichment and the future" (p. 155).[56]

II. Our quest to conquer the animal word is making for inferior breeds of many species. Case in point, our trying to produce pure and pristine animals (such as dogs, cows, chickens, pigs) by controlling and manipulating the breeding of various species and limiting the breeding of other species that we judge and perceive to be ugly and inferior. Yet these supposed pure and pristine animals usually come with all manner of defects, diseases, and illnesses.

Against Purity

In the same way that inbreeding among human populations can increase the frequency of normally rare genes that cause diseases, the selective breeding that created the hundreds of modern dog breeds has put purebred dogs at risk for a large number of health problems, affecting both body and behavior.

Some conditions are directly related to the features breeders have sought to perpetuate among their dogs. As they deliberately manipulated the appearance of dogs to create or accentuate physical characteristics that were considered aesthetically pleasing, like the flat face of a bulldog or low-slung eyelids of a Bloodhound, breeders also created physical disabilities. The excessively wrinkled skin of the Chinese Shar-Pei causes frequent skin infection; Bulldogs and other flat-faced

---

[56] United Nations Education and Scientific Organization (2005). *Towards knowledge societies.* http://unesdoc.unesco.org/images/0014/001418/141843e.pdf

(or brachycephalic) breeds such as the Pekingese have breathing problems because of their set-back noses and shortened air passages; Bloodhounds suffer chronic eye irritation and infection.

The unnaturally large and small sizes of other breeds encourage different problems. For example, toy and miniature breeds often suffer from dislocating kneecaps and heart problems are more common among small dogs. Giant dogs such as Mastiffs, Saint Bernards, and Great Danes are nearly too big for their own good. Researchers have found a striking correlation between a dog's large size and a frequency of orthopedic problems like hip dysplasia. Large dogs are often prone to heat prostration because they can't cool down their bodies (tiny dogs, by contrast, have a hard time staying warm), and because of the massive weight they must support, these breeds are prone to malignant bone tumors in their legs. Meanwhile, the huge head and narrow hips of the Bulldog can necessitate that their pups must be born by Caesarean section.

Other health problems among purebreds are the product of both inbreeding and bad genetic luck. The genes responsible for many genetic diseases are "recessive," which means that two copies of a damaged gene, one from the mother and one from the father, must be present in an individual for the disease to occur. Individuals that carry only one copy of the disease gene don't have the condition, and are carriers of the disease. Normally, because disease genes are relatively rare, it is unlikely that both the mother and the father will be carriers, and even less likely that they'll both give the disease gene to their offspring. But that's not the case for purebred dog breeds, where genetically similar individuals are intentionally mated, increasing the concentration of disease genes. It's like stacking a deck of cards with ten extra aces and ten extra face cards; the loaded deck increases your chance of hitting blackjack in a game of 21-but what you "win" might be allergies or a predisposition to cancer.[57]

---

[57] Excerpted from *Dogs That Changed The World.* http://www.pbs.org/wnet/nature/episodes/dogs-that-changed-the-world/selective-breeding-problems/1281/

III. Our quest to conquer the natural world is eroding plant diversity and making for the entry of dangerous chemicals (pesticides and herbicides) in the food chain. Case in point, our trying to produce pure and pristine lawns and gardens by vanquishing various plants and species that we judge and perceive to be ugly and inferior. In the end, however, this loss of plant diversity threatens the well-being of all of humanity.

Ending Diversity

A decline in the diversity of farmed plants and livestock breeds is gathering pace, threatening future food supplies for the world's growing population, the head of a new United Nations panel on biodiversity said on Monday.

Preserving neglected animal breeds and plants was necessary as they could have genes resistant to future diseases or to shifts in the climate to warmer temperatures, more droughts or downpours, Zakri Abdul Hamid said.

"The loss of biodiversity is happening faster and everywhere, even among farm animals," Zakri told a conference of 450 experts in Trondheim, central Norway, in his first speech as founding chair of the U.N. biodiversity panel.

Many traditional breeds of cows, sheep or goats have fallen out of favour, often because they yield less meat or milk than new breeds. Globalisation also means that people's food preferences narrow down to fewer plants.

Zakri said there were 30,000 edible plants but that just 30 crops accounted for 95 percent of the energy in human food that is dominated by rice, wheat, maize, millet and sorghum.

He said it was "more important than ever to have a large genetic pool to enable organisms to withstand and adapt to new conditions." That would help to ensure food for a global population set to reach 9 billion by 2050 from 7 billion now.

Zakri noted that the U.N.'s Food and Agriculture Organization estimated last year that 22 percent of the world's livestock breeds were at risk of extinction. That means there are fewer than 1,000 animals in each breed.

The extinctions of some domesticated animals and plants was happening in tandem with accelerating losses of wild species caused by factors such as deforestation, expansion of cities, pollution and climate change, he said.

Irene Hoffmann, chief of the FAO's animal genetic resources branch, told Reuters that eight percent of livestock breeds had already become extinct.

In 2010, governments set goals including halting extinction of known threatened species by 2020 and expanding the area set aside in parks or protected areas for wildlife to 17 percent of the Earth's land surface from about 13 percent now.[58]

IV. Our quest to conquer the biological world (e.g., germs, viruses) is making for the rise of new dangerous species (superbugs). Case in point, our trying to have our environs (homes, playgrounds, offices, and so forth) free of all viruses and microbes that we judge and perceive to be a threat to our health. Yet all this sanitizing and disinfecting is only making our situation increasingly perilous by

---

[58] Excerpted from Doyle, A. (2013, May 27). Biodiversity Loss Becoming Major Threat For Farmed Plants And Livestock Breeds. *Reuters.* http://www.huffingtonpost.com/2013/05/27/biodiversity-loss-plants-animals-livestock_n_3341872.html

creating new strains of viruses and microbes that are immune to our chemicals.

Deadly & Untreatable

A family of "nightmare" superbugs — untreatable and often deadly — is spreading through hospitals across the USA, and doctors fear that it may soon be too late to stop them, senior health officials said Tuesday.

"These are nightmare bacteria that present a triple threat," said Thomas Frieden, director of the Centers for Disease Control and Prevention. "They're resistant to nearly all antibiotics. They have high mortality rates, killing half of people with serious infections. And they can spread their resistance to other bacteria."

So far, this particular class of superbug, called carbapenem-resistant Enterobacteriaceae, or CRE, has been found only in hospitals or nursing homes, rather than in the community, Frieden said. But officials sounded the alarm partly because, if the bacteria's spread isn't contained soon, even common infections could become untreatable.

These superbugs are "the biggest threat to patient safety in the hospital that we have," said Costi Sifri, an infectious disease physician and hospital epidemiologist at the University of Virginia Health System. "Unfortunately, it doesn't seem like anything is slowing their spread."

In the first half of 2012, nearly 200 hospitals treated at least one of these infections, Frieden said. About 4% of hospitals have had at least one patient with CRE, along with 18% of long-term, acute-care hospitals, the CDC said.

Those numbers could underestimate the scope of the problem, however. There are no reliable national data on CRE infections. There is no national requirement that hospitals and other health care facilities report CRE cases. CDC officials noted Tuesday that only six states require hospitals and other health care facilities to report CRE infections.

Perhaps the greatest threat from CRE is its ability to share its resistance genes with other bacteria. So although CRE's spread is somewhat limited today, it could potentially share its resistance with far more common bacteria, such as E. coli, Frieden said.

If that happened, common conditions affecting millions of Americans, which are now treated with antibiotics — such as diarrhea, urinary tract infections, respiratory conditions and pneumonia — could become untreatable.

"It's not very often that our scientists come to me and say, 'We have a very serious problem and we need to say something to save lives,' but that is what is happening," said Frieden, who outlined a six-step plan for hospitals, called "Detect and protect."

"We can't afford to wait until a large-scale outbreak occurs to fight these dangerous bacteria," said Sara Cosgrove, who serves on the board of Society for Healthcare Epidemiology of America. "Excessive antibiotic use combined with failure of health care workers to wash hands before and after caring for patients allows these bugs to develop and spread."

There is little chance that an effective drug to kill CRE bacteria will be produced in the coming years. Manufacturers have no new antibiotics in development that show promise, according to federal officials and industry experts, and there's little financial incentive because the bacteria adapt quickly to resist new drugs.[59]

---

[59] Excerpted from Szabo, L., & Eisler, P. (2013, March 6). CDC sounds alarm on deadly, untreatable superbugs. *USA Today.* http://www.usatoday.com/story/news/nation/2013/03/05/superbugs-infections hospitals/1965133/

V. Our quest to demystify how the world works and, consequently, gain dominion over the world makes for all manner of illusions and delusions.

The Beginning Of Inquiry

There is concern that research, left to itself, driven by its implacable reductionism, will quickly penetrate all the great mysteries and we will be left with nothing to contemplate but the nasty little details of a monstrous machine. There is a genuine apprehension that science may be taking the meaning out of life.

But if you concentrate on science, it is in real life not like this at all. We are nowhere near comprehension. The greatest achievements in the science . . . are themselves the sources of more puzzlement than human beings have ever experienced. Indeed, it is likely that the twentieth century will be looked back at as the time when science provided the first close glimpse of the profundity of human ignorance. We have not reached solutions; we have only begun to discover how to ask questions.

Science is founded on uncertainty. Each time we learn something new and surprising, the astonishment comes with the realization that we were wrong before. The body of science is not, as it is sometimes thought, a huge coherent mass of facts, neatly arranged in sequence, each one attached to the next by a logical string. In truth, whenever we discover a new fact it involves the elimination of old ones. We are always, as it turns out, fundamentally in error.

I cannot think of a single field in biology or medicine in which we can claim genuine understanding, and it seems to me the more we learn about living creatures, especially ourselves, the stranger life becomes. I do not understand modern physics at all, but my colleagues who know a lot about the physics of very small things, like the particles in atoms, or very large things, like the universe, seem to be running into one queerness after another, from puzzle to puzzle.

The sense of strangeness and ambiguity is the best evidence that science is working. The world is not a simple place, nor are we simple instruments. We should have known this long ago, but we found it easier in earlier centuries to tell tales to each other; powerfully explanatory but based on pure guesswork, and generally mistaken. Now that we have made a beginning of sorts, it is becoming clear that nothing, is clear. I believe that the exploration of nature, given the spectacular human gift of insatiable curiosity, will never be concluded. I cannot for the life of me imagine a time when all your questions will do more than, raise new questions, with new astonishments for answers.

It is a risky business, science. Not only do you have to start your work by assuming the existence of wrongness, you must count on a very high probability of being wrong in your own experiments, running into dead ends, finishing the work with that greatest of scientific disasters, a "trivial" observation. It takes the greatest skill, and a measure of courage, to turn your imagination completely loose, and this is the mandatory first step. You make up a story to explain whatever it is that you are curious about and then you design an experiment to test the story, building in all the controls that you can think of in order to make sure that your wish to be right, just this once, will not influence the outcome. This, by the way, is where the greatest danger lies: you can wish too hard for it to be a garden path and overlook the plainest evidences of a blind alley. I do not know of a chancier profession. . . .

We know a lot about the structure and function of the cells and fibers of the human brain, but we haven't the ghost of an idea about how this extraordinary organ works to produce awareness; the nature of consciousness is a scientific problem, but still an unapproachable one. We can make good educated guesses about the origin of life on this planet: it must have started, we think, as single-celled creatures resembling today's bacteria, but we have no way of tracking back to the events preceding this first cell, nor can we lay out an orderly scheme for explaining the nearly four billion years of evolutionary process from such a cell to ourselves.

We do not know how the first cells of an embryo, starting from the fusion of an egg and a sperm, sort themselves out with infallible precision into the systems of differentiated cells of a baby, each cell in possession of all the information needed for the formation of a complete baby but with most of that information switched off so that it can only become, say, a skin cell or a brain cell. We do not know how normal cells are transformed into cancer cells; we know the names of some of the chemicals, viruses and types of radiation that can launch this process, but the nature of the process itself eludes us.

We know that songbirds have centers on the left sides of their brains for the generation of birdsong, and we suspect that this may somehow be related to the lateralization of speech centers in our own brains, but we do not understand language itself. Indeed, language is so incomprehensible a problem that the language we use for discussing the matter is itself becoming incomprehensible. We do not know what holds us together as a social species; it is a mystery that we are so dependent on each other, in search all our lives for affection, and yet so willing to destroy each other when assembled in larger groups; the failure of nations to conduct their affairs with anything resembling the humanity we expect from each other as individuals is, somehow, a biological problem still beyond our reach. We do not understand the process of dying, nor can we say anything clear, for sure, about what happens to human thought after death.

In short, we are an ignorant species, new to the earth, still juvenile . . . we have a long way to go.[60]

---

[60] Excerpted from Thomas, L. (Chancellor of the Memorial Sloan-Kettering Cancer Center) (1980, October). On Science and Uncertainty. *Discover.* http://www.philosophy-religion.org/handouts/uncertainty.htm

VI. Our ambition to produce pure and pristine foods by increasingly processing, pasteurizing, and reengineering our foods so as to remove those features and elements that we judge and perceive to be undesirable is only making our foods unhealthy.

Killing Foods

1) Processed foods are highly addictive. Your body processes whole foods much differently than it does refined, processed, and heavily-modified "junk" foods. Processed foods tend to over stimulate the production of dopamine, also known as the "pleasure" neurotransmitter, which makes you crave them constantly. Your body ends up not being able to resist the temptation to continue eating junk foods in excess, which can lead to obesity and other health problems.

2) Processed foods often contain phosphates that destroy your organs, bones. Many processed foods contain phosphate additives that augment taste, texture, and shelf-life. But these additives are known to cause health problems like rapid aging, kidney deterioration and weak bones, according to the Rodale Institute.

3) Processed foods cause chronic inflammation. One of the leading causes of chronic illness today is inflammation. . . . studies continue to show that refined sugars, processed flours, vegetable oils, and many other nasty ingredients commonly found in processed foods are largely responsible for this inflammation epidemic.

4) Processed foods ruin digestion. Because they have been stripped of their natural fibers, enzymes, vitamins, and other nutrients, processed foods tend to wreak havoc on the digestive tract. Chronic consumption of such foods can throw your internal ecosystem off balance, harming beneficial bacteria and exposing your system to infection.

5) Processed foods destroy your mind. If you suffer from chronic bouts of brain "fog," or have difficulty concentrating and thinking normally, chances are your diet has something to do with it. . . . A recent study out of Oxford University lends credence to this possibility, having found that junk food consumption can cause people to become angry and irritable. Nutrient-dense whole foods, on the other hand, can help level out your mood, sustain your energy levels, and leave you feeling calmer and more collected.

6) Processed foods are loaded with GMOs. The basic buildings blocks of most processed foods on the market today are derived from laboratories, not nature. Genetically-modified organisms (GMOs), which have been linked to infertility, organ damage, gastrointestinal disorders, and cancer, are prolific in processed foods. Excess consumption of these poisons promotes weight gain, acidifies your blood, and can even permanently alter the composition and function of your intestinal flora.

7) Processed foods are loaded with pesticides. In order to effectively grow the GMOs used in processed foods, conventional farmers have to apply Roundup (glyphosate) and other pesticides and herbicides, many of which end up in the final product. According to data compiled by Rodale, breakfast cereals alone have been found to contain up to 70 different types of pesticides, including warehouse fumigation chemicals and other residues.[61]

VII. Our quest to make communication pure and pristine by removing noise and confusion undermines the conflict, dissent, and tension that are necessary for diversity and a vibrant democracy.

A Case Study
Redefining Noise & Confusion

What does it mean when a university manual titled *"Building a Culture of Respect, Diversity and Inclusion"* recommends first and foremost that we should avoid doing or saying "anything that could be perceived as harassing"? Indeed, when anything can possibly be perceived as harassing, and when the manual states that all that makes for a valid complaint is the impact of action rather than the intention, and when "I never meant to offend you" is no legal defense, this recommendation

---

[61] Excerpted from Huff, E. A. (2013, April 2). Nine reasons to never eat processed foods again. *Natural News*. http://www.naturalnews.com/039743_processed_foods_eating_reasons.html

makes sense. We are left with the impression that in order to achieve diversity, respect, and inclusion, less communication is best. What then becomes the case for communication studies as a legitimate discipline when the world is supposedly better off with less communication? What also becomes the case for communication in an increasingly plural and multicultural?

The National Communication Association's (NCA) official description of the communication process makes plain that communication involves displacing confusion. *"A communicator encodes (e.g., puts thoughts into words and gestures), then transmits the message via a channel (e.g., speaking, email, text message) to the other communicator(s) who then decode the message (e.g., take the words and apply meaning to them). The message may encounter noise (e.g., any physical, psychological, or physiological distraction or interference), which could prevent the message from being received or fully understood as the sender intended."* We supposedly achieve communication by displacing noise (confusion). Confusion is supposedly the nemesis of communication. Thus most of communication theory, inquiry, and pedagogy are about identifying the most effective means of removing, managing, and lessening noise and confusion.

According to Uncertainty Reduction Theory, probably the most popular communication theory, communication emerges from the reduction of uncertainty. But removing noise/uncertainty/confusion from communication is all but impossible. In a world of boundless ambiguity, confusion is a constant. Even our best descriptions and explanations will be laden with noise, ambiguity, and uncertainty. However, difference resides in noise. Without confusion, communication would be impossible. Confusion sustains and catalyzes communication. It also organically destabilizes our interpretations and descriptions, and, in doing so, ensures that doubt continues to have a place in human affairs. Noise is difference, as difference is that which is uncategorizable, indefinable, and untranslatable. In other words, noise is about what we are unable and incapable of naming, categorizing, and understanding. In this way, noise is always bound up with communication, as what we are capable of understanding will always be finite. Or, put differently, there is always noise in communication. If communication is about what is spoken, noise is about what is silenced. If communication is about what is symbolized and languaged, noise is about that which refuses to be symbolized and languaged. That noise is bound up with communication means that difference is also bound up in communication. How much difference we are capable of cultivating depends on how much communication we are capable of achieving. Both share a common fate. However, how much communication we are capable of creating begins with how we define communication. If we continue to define communication as inherently a symbolic and linguistic activity, this impedes the expansion of communication, and, subsequently, that of difference. Defining communication this way assumes and encourages the idea that symbolic and linguistic convergence is necessary for communication. Conversely, symbolic and linguistic divergence presumably thwarts communication. In this symbolic and linguistic model of communication, difference emerges as a threat to communication. It must therefore be either removed or managed. Either way, the noise, the difference, must be dealt with for the sake of good things happening. In short, this model puts difference in an irreconcilable conflict with communication. It is inherently hostile to difference, and also perpetuates the idea that difference needs to be removed or lessened in order for good things to happen. We are to assume that in order for communication to flourish, we must vanquish noise, vanquish difference. Yet when we limit noise we limit communication.

An increasingly plural and multicultural world needs models of communication that embrace both noise and communication, and also recognize that both dwell within each other. We therefore need models that view communication as something other than a symbolic and linguistic activity. We also need models that release us from the tyranny of convergence, as in viewing communication in terms of achieving common understanding. After all, why should we devalue what we are unable to share and understand? How did such things come to have no place in communication? But such is the tyranny of convergence that pervades communication studies. Anything we perceive as a threat to convergence must either be removed or neutralized. We expect convergence. We assume that communication is about assimilating and neutralizing difference. It is about bringing order to chaos. With enough transacting, communication will presumably and eventually arise from confusion. Communication becomes a distilling process—the goal is to remove the elements (noise) that supposedly pollute and contaminate communication. But as with any distilling process, nothing lives in the end. The demise of noise is the demise of communication. Indeed, in our unrelenting quest to conquer noise, we have impoverished communication. Communication is now about skill and competency rather than integrity and character. We view communication as a tool for expressing ourselves and advancing our interests rather than a process where we create ourselves and our worlds. We should therefore be in no way surprised that a university manual about *"Building a Culture of Respect, Diversity and Inclusion"* recommends first and foremost that we avoid doing or saying "anything that could be perceived as harassing." We are to assume that cultivating diversity has nothing to do with communication. In fact, communication supposedly threatens diversity. Thus for the sake of promoting diversity, less communication is presumably best. But again, without communication, what kind of diversity is possible? All that remains is a diversity that is devoid of life and purpose. That is, all that remains is a caricature of diversity. This diversity can be assimilated and comfortably included because it poses no threat to anything. Indeed, besides doing the bidding of the status quo, this diversity works to protect the status quo. It does so by calling for the end of communication, as in the rise of speech codes and other movements that threaten communication with sanction and retribution. Only the orthodoxy will be tolerated. There shall be no dissent, no diversity of worldviews. Either submit and conform to our rationality and sensibility, or face sanction and retribution. Yet how could this kind of conformity be an expression of diversity?

Epilogue

No epistemology can reveal the complete nature of anything. The reason being that every epistemology is a human creation, reflecting our own physical and historical limits. We are only capable of perceiving and understanding so much. In the end, human beings must believe, and to believe is to acknowledge our limits. What we believe shapes how we perceive and make sense of things. This reality means that there are always other ways of understanding things and what we understand and label as *Truth* will never be complete. Changing how we perceive the world involves changing what we believe.

At the foundation of colonialism is a set of beliefs—beliefs about what being human means, as in believing that human potentiality is measurable and quantifiable; beliefs about the world, as in believing that the world is outside and separate from us; beliefs about what makes for a good society, as in believing commonality and homogeneity make for peace and prosperity. History will record that these beliefs have served us poorly.

Our prosperity and even survival will depend on us cultivating a new set of beliefs. What now seems self-evident is that the world values diversity. Life flourishes through diversity. We need new foundational beliefs that reflect this fact. This includes the possibility of believing that the origins of communication reside outside of evolutionary necessity. Put differently, what of the possibility that the origins of communication have nothing to do with evolutionary necessity, and thus communication is merely an evolutionary tool to promote organization and coordination? That is, what of the possibility of the origins residing elsewhere? Also, what of the possibility that the purpose of communication resides in divergence rather than convergence? That is, why should understanding be the limits of communication? Why should the only communication that is tolerable is that which promotes understanding or is capable of being understood?

Diversity means the promotion and cultivation of different narratives. We need many new narratives of communication. This diversity begins with us creating spaces for the possibility of these narratives. We can do this in different ways as these spaces are physical but also ideological, pedagogical, and epistemological in nature. Integral to us creating these spaces for new narratives is our owning of and acknowledging our own colonialism.

Afterword

This book is my story of communication studies. I did my under-graduate and all my graduate training at historically black colleges. I was always a communication major. I used the same texts that were used in other communication departments. I was introduced early to the transactional model of communication and never once given the impression that there were *Other* ways of defining communication. Nor did I ever encounter any criticisms of this model of communica-tion. I also had to learn the same set of communication theories and all the ways to compare and evaluate different theories. I never was required to read anything about the problem with theory and theoriz-ing, especially for peoples who have been historically marginalized and brutalized.

Nor was I ever introduced to any stories of communication and any communication knowledge from African, Latin American, Asian, and indigenous peoples. In my graduate training I was required to take a set of quantitative courses and even a quantitative certification test to sat-isfy my requirements for graduation. I still know of no other communi-cation department that has such a test. But in none of my undergradu-ate and graduate curriculums was there ever a qualitative course, and for sure there was no method course that was outside the quantitative/ qualitative axis. Many of my professors were wonderful human beings and never would have discouraged my pursuit of *Other* ways of framing communication research. But there were no tools and training to make such an exploration possible.

Even in my graduate training I never probed the notion of epistemology. I was left with the impression that the theories and methodologies found in communication studies had no historical context and thereby involved no human-making processes. Coming from historically black colleges I was always to believe that the struggle was about the inclusion of peoples who have been historically excluded and marginalized. It was specifically about challenging the status quo in communication studies to recognize that race matters, culture matters. Only much later was I to realize that this enterprise would never disrupt anything and was inherently incapable of doing so. It was compromised from the start.

The status quo in communication studies always knew that race and culture were important. There was always race and culture in communication studies. Both were in plain sight in the theories, pedagogies, and methodologies found in communication curriculums. The Western/European epistemology that frames communication studies has always been raced and cultured, and will always remain of a certain race and culture. The rest of us will remain of *this* race and culture as long we continue to embody this epistemology. This is why our enterprise to be included and recognized will never disrupt anything. This is also why the National Communication Association could add, after much clamoring by minority members, a new journal (*Journal of International and Intercultural Communication*) that promises to deal with race and culture without any fear of disruption. Nearly all the articles that appear in this journal use the same theories and methodologies found in nearly all communication curriculums and hold to the same standards of academic excellence found in every other communication journal. All that tends to be different is the race and culture of the persons being analyzed and theorized about. This is what the struggle for inclusion continues to look like in communication studies.

Journal of International and Intercultural Communication (JIIC) serves as a primary outlet for original research on international and intercultural communication. The journal showcases diverse perspectives and methods, including qualitative, quantitative, critical and textual approaches. It addresses an international readership and features research conducted in a wide range of locations by diverse groups of scholars.

Articles published in JIIC should be theoretically informed and sophisticated, relate broadly to socially significant issues, and be methodologically and argumentatively rigorous. All submissions to the journal will be peer reviewed and all special issues and forums will be preceded by an open call for papers.

Both theoretical and empirical submissions are therefore welcomed from authors across the world that expand our understanding of international and intercultural communication theories, issues and practices, in such contexts as: democracy, the environment, gender and sexuality, globalization, health, identity, media, organizing, pedagogy, postcolonialism, technology, transnationalism, and work-places, among others.

Upon completing my graduate studies I got an appointment at one of the largest and most prestigious communication departments in the United States. The Dean of the college directed the department to make a diversity hire. The department, as with nearly every other major communication department, was exclusively White. Soon after taking up my appointment, I, along with all the new hires, had an orientation session with the chair of the department regarding the requirements for tenure and promotion. We were given a tenure and promotion document that listed the exact demands for tenure and promotion. There was nothing in the document about teaching. Tenure and promotion was a numbers game. Only by making the publication numbers in the most reputable communication journals was tenure and promotion possible.

Communication journals were ranked by levels of rejection rates. The higher the rejection rate, the higher the ranking of the journal. Nothing in the tenure and promotion document was without a measurable value. Although teaching had no place in the tenure and promotion process, quality of teaching was still measured by quantitative course evaluations. So even teaching was reduced to numbers. In both research and teaching numbers would be used to measure our excellence and accomplishments. The best researchers and teachers had the best numbers. Then there were the rankings of the different departments in the college. This also was determined by research output: the department with the most annual publications had the highest standing. Then there was the ranking of communication departments by the National Communication Association. Finally, there was the ranking of individual professors by the association that was assumed to reflect status and accomplishments. This list is exclusively based on research output, and as with every other ranking that showed the department doing well, would be posted prominently in the department. The list was always dominated by persons who did quantitative research. In private conversations the persons from our department who were on the list were referred to as "the quants." There were endless quants in the department.

But this is what hegemony looks like in communication studies. Whether in research or teaching, only numbers matter. Make the numbers, and the keys to the kingdom will be yours. This normally means developing a research program that would make for quick and successive publications. It all begins with acquiring a set of "rich" datasets that lend for different kinds of quantitative analyses. Every analysis makes for a different publication, culminating in a final analysis of all the previous analyses for a final publication. This is commonly called data-driven research and it is the most reliable and popular path to tenure and promotion at the most prestigious communication departments. The writing of the papers must be devoid of any passion or emotion. There must be no politics so as to avoid antagonizing journal editors and anonymous referees. The paper should read as if it was written by a machine. Soon after meeting with the chair of my department I met with my assigned mentor who advised that I begin acquiring a good deal of datasets. I was to stay away from theory until I got tenure and promotion. That stuff was "hard to publish" and I had a short period to make "the numbers" for tenure and promotion.

Yet I still decided to do differently. Although I had the quantitative training to follow the advised model for tenure and promotion, and I was surrounded by many of the most accomplished quantitative researchers whom I could tap for help, I found it impossible to submit. There were simply too many questions I had about communication that I could find no answers to in communication studies. Since graduate school I was struggling with these questions. Never did I know that pursuing these questions would become my life's work. I eventually moved on from this department, which of this writing is yet to tenure and promote a Black, Latino, or Native American professor. Such is the status of diversity in most supposedly prestigious communication departments. However, as much as achieving this kind of diversity is important, the real problem that plagues communication studies is the lack of epistemological diversity—diversity in perceiving and understanding the world.

In order for the race and culture of *Others* to matter in communication studies the struggle has to begin at the epistemological level. We cannot merely be about using the current stock of theories and methodologies to analyze minority populations, revising existing theories to account for race and culture, or even articulating supposedly new communication theories about race and culture. We have to be willing to cast aside the communication theories, pedagogies, and methodologies that are of the Western/European epistemology, and be ready to forge new epistemologies that promote new ways of defining, teaching, and understanding communication. Yet this enterprise cannot merely be about the rise of epistemologies that reflect different races, cultures, and heritages. It must ultimately be about the rise of new epistemologies that contribute to the making of a life-affirming world that serves the interest of *all* peoples. Only with the making of such a world do all human beings—regardless of our differences—have any chance of life, peace, and prosperity.

About the Author

Amardo Rodriguez (Howard University, Ph.D.) is a Laura J. and L. Douglas Meredith Professor in the Department of Communication and Rhetorical Studies at Syracuse University. His research and teaching interests explore the potentiality of emergent conceptions of communication that foreground moral, existential, and spiritual assumptions about the human condition to redefine and enlarge contemporary understandings of democracy, diversity, and community.

Made in the USA
San Bernardino, CA
04 September 2015